In A.I. We Trust

———————

In A.I. We Trust

———

John Q.A. Smith

Books Written By The Author

Conversations With An A.I. Program

In A.I. We Trust

First paperback edition 2023

Paperback ISBN: 9798374928419

In A.I. We Trust

Please note that all responses (not in bold) were the actual responses that were provided. No attempts have been made to correct any spelling mistakes, punctuations or faulty information.

Who is the single most influential human being ever?

The question of who the single most influential human being ever is a matter of opinion and perspective. There are many individuals throughout history who have had a profound impact on the world and humanity.

Jesus of Nazareth, who is considered the central figure of Christianity and has had a profound influence on the development of Western civilization.

How could Jesus be the most influential human being ever if he was a God?

According to Christian theology, Jesus is believed to be fully God and fully human, having both a divine and human nature united in one person. As God, Jesus is believed to have existed eternally, and as the son of God, his influence is considered to be eternal and limitless. As a human being, Jesus lived among people, performed miracles and teachings that changed the lives of many, and his message and teachings continue to inspire and guide people today.

The belief in Jesus as both God and man is a fundamental tenet of Christianity, and it is this belief that has led to Jesus being considered the most influential human being in history. His teachings and message continue to shape the lives of billions of people around the world, and his message of love, forgiveness, and redemption has led to the formation of one of the largest and most widespread religions in the world. Additionally, Jesus' impact has been felt not only in the religious sphere, but also in art, literature, philosophy and even in politics.

In summary, Jesus' influence as a God is eternal, and as a human being, his teachings, message, and actions have had a profound impact on humanity. These aspects of Jesus make him one of the most influential figures in world history.

In Christianity, Jesus is believed to be both fully human and fully God. This doctrine, known as the hypostatic union, holds that Jesus has two natures, one human and one divine, united in one person without confusion, alteration, division, or separation. This belief is central to Christian theology and is a fundamental tenet of the Christian faith.

How many Gods are there?

Different religions and belief systems have different understandings of the nature and number of gods. In monotheistic religions such as Christianity, Judaism, and Islam, there is only one God who is considered to be the creator and ruler of the universe. In polytheistic religions, such as Hinduism and ancient Greek religion, there are many gods, each with their own specific domains and responsibilities. Some belief systems like animism, ancestor worship, and shamanism, gods are often spirits or ancestors that are considered to have control over certain aspects of the natural world.

It's important to note that what one person may consider as "God" may not be the same as another person's understanding of the term, as different cultures and belief systems have different concepts of the divine. It's also important to understand that people's beliefs on this topic are often deeply personal and can be influenced by many factors, such as culture, upbringing, education and personal experiences.

Where does the idea of Gods come from?

The origin of gods is a complex and multifaceted topic that varies greatly depending on the religion or belief system in question.

In monotheistic religions such as Christianity, Judaism, and Islam, God is believed to be the creator of the universe and is considered to be the source of all things. God is considered to be eternal, unchanging and self-existent, and not being created by any other being.

In polytheistic religions, such as Hinduism, ancient Greek religion, and many ancient cultures, gods are often believed to have originated from the natural world, such as the sun, the moon, and the earth. They are often believed to have been born from the forces of nature, or from the actions of other gods. Some gods were considered to be the offspring of other gods, or the result of a union between a god and a mortal.

In animism, ancestor worship, and shamanism, gods are often considered to be spirits or ancestors that are considered to have control over certain aspects of the natural world. They are often considered to be the spirits of deceased ancestors, nature spirits, or other entities that are believed to inhabit the natural world.

It's important to note that the origins of gods are often intertwined with the origin stories and cosmologies of different cultures and belief systems, and these stories often serve as explanations for the natural world, the human condition, and the relationship between the divine and the mortal

What evidence exists that Gods are real?

The question of the existence of gods is a complex and highly debated topic that has been the subject of much philosophical and religious inquiry throughout history. Different religions and belief systems have their own unique understandings of the nature and existence of gods.

In monotheistic religions such as Christianity, Judaism, and Islam, the existence of God is often considered to be a matter of faith, and it is believed that God's existence cannot be proven or disproven through scientific or empirical means. The belief in God is often based on religious texts, personal experiences, and faith.

In polytheistic religions, such as Hinduism, ancient Greek religion, and many ancient cultures, the existence of gods is often considered to be a matter of tradition, and it is believed that

8

gods are part of the natural world and can be observed in the forces of nature.

In animism, ancestor worship, and shamanism, gods are often considered to be spirits or ancestors that are considered to have control over certain aspects of the natural world. They are often considered to be the spirits of deceased ancestors, nature spirits, or other entities that are believed to inhabit the natural world.

It's important to note that the existence of gods is not something that can be proven or disproven through scientific means, as gods are not considered to be physical entities that can be observed or measured in the same way that scientific experiments are conducted. People's beliefs on this topic are often deeply personal, and are influenced by many factors, such as culture, upbringing, education and personal experiences.

If Gods are real but we can't see or communicate directly with them, how did humans know that they are real?

The question of how humans know that gods are real is a topic of much debate and speculation among theologians and philosophers. Different religions and belief systems have their own unique understandings of the nature and existence of gods.

Many monotheistic religions, such as Christianity, Judaism, and Islam, believe that God is not a physical being that can be seen or communicated with in the same way that humans interact with other physical entities. Instead, God is believed to be a spiritual being that can be experienced through faith, religious texts, and personal revelation.

Many polytheistic religions, such as Hinduism, ancient Greek religion, and many ancient cultures, gods are often considered to be present in the natural world, and can be observed in the forces of nature, such as the sun, the moon, and the earth. They are often believed to have been born from the forces of nature, or from the actions of other gods.

In animism, ancestor worship, and shamanism, gods are often considered to be spirits or ancestors that are considered to have control over certain aspects of the natural world. They are often considered to be the spirits of deceased ancestors, nature

9

spirits, or other entities that are believed to inhabit the natural world.

It's important to note that the concept of God and the belief in their existence is a complex and multifaceted topic that varies greatly depending on the religion or belief system in question. People's beliefs on this topic are often deeply personal, and are influenced by many factors, such as culture, upbringing, education and personal experiences.

Are Gods not simply created from human imagination?

The idea that gods are simply a product of human imagination is a perspective held by some philosophers and scholars. They argue that gods are a human invention, created as an explanation for natural phenomena that people did not understand. The human need for control and the fear of the unknown, led people to create gods and goddesses to explain everything from the weather to their own mortality.

Other scholars point out that belief in gods predates recorded history and is found in every culture around the world. They argue that the idea of gods is not simply a human invention, but instead, it's a universal human experience that can't be explained by human imagination alone.

It's also important to note that the concept of gods is complex and multifaceted, and different religions and belief systems have their own unique understandings of the nature and existence of gods. Some believe that gods are real, eternal entities that exist independent of human imagination. Others believe that gods are simply symbolic representations of natural forces and human emotions.

In summary, whether gods are a product of human imagination or not is a topic of ongoing debate and different people have different perspectives on this topic.

If God is eternal and the universe had a beginning, what was God doing before the universe was created?

The question of what God was doing before the universe was created is a topic of much debate and speculation among theologians and philosophers. Many monotheistic religions, such as Christianity, Judaism, and Islam, believe that God is eternal and not subject to time in the same way that the universe is. This means that God is not limited by time and therefore the concept of "before" the creation of the universe does not apply to God.

One way to understand this is that God is considered as the creator of time and space, and therefore, the idea of time does not apply to God as it does to the created universe.

Additionally, some religious traditions propose that God has always existed and that there was no "before" for God. The belief is that God is eternal, self-existent, and uncreated. This belief is rooted in the idea that God is beyond human comprehension and that our human understanding of time does not apply to God.

It's important to note that different religions and belief systems have different understandings of the nature and existence of God, and this question is a complex topic that has been the subject of much philosophical and religious inquiry throughout history.

Which God is the most influential to humans?

The most influential God to humans varies greatly depending on the culture and belief system in question.

In monotheistic religions such as Christianity, Judaism and Islam, the God of Abraham is considered to be the most influential as it is the creator of the universe and the source of all things.

In Hinduism, the most influential god is considered to be Lord Vishnu, who is considered to be the preserver of the universe, and is often depicted as holding a conch shell and a discus.

In Buddhism, the most influential god is considered to be the Buddha, who is not considered to be a god in the traditional sense but rather an enlightened being who achieved Nirvana and taught the path to enlightenment

In ancient Egyptian religion, the most influential gods were considered to be Amun-Ra, the creator god, and Osiris, the god of the afterlife.

It's important to note that the most influential God to humans may change over time and across different cultures and societies. Additionally, the concept of God can be interpreted differently by different people, and people's beliefs on this topic are often deeply personal, and are influenced by many factors, such as culture, upbringing, education and personal experiences.

Who was Jesus?

Jesus of Nazareth, also known as Jesus Christ, is the central figure of Christianity and one of the most important figures in world history. He is believed by Christians to be the Son of God and the Messiah (or savior) prophesied in the Old Testament. According to the New Testament, Jesus was born to the Virgin Mary in Bethlehem and was baptized by John the Baptist. He then began his public ministry, during which he performed a number of miracles, such as healing the sick and feeding the hungry, and gave many teachings, including the Sermon on the Mount. He was eventually arrested, tried, and sentenced to death by crucifixion, an event that is known as the Passion. Christians believe that three days after his death, Jesus rose from the dead, an event known as the Resurrection. After his resurrection, Jesus appeared to his disciples and many others before ascending to heaven. The belief in Jesus' death and resurrection is the cornerstone of the Christian faith and the foundation of the Christian doctrine of salvation.

What does Jesus represent to human beings?

Jesus represents different things to different people, but for Christians, he is the central figure of their faith and represents salvation and redemption. According to Christian belief, Jesus lived a perfect and sinless life, and willingly died on the cross to atone for the sins of humanity. Christians believe that by accepting Jesus as their personal savior, they can have their sins forgiven and be granted eternal life in heaven. In addition, Jesus is considered as an example of how to live a good life, teaching to love, compassion, kindness, forgiveness, and humility. Jesus is also seen as a teacher, a prophet, and a leader. He is also considered as a model of service and self-sacrifice, He is also seen as the embodiment of God's love for humanity.

Is there evidence Jesus Christ ever existed?

Jesus of Nazareth, also known as Jesus Christ, is a central figure in Christianity and is considered by Christians to be the Son of God and the Messiah (or savior) prophesied in the Old Testament. The historical existence of Jesus is attested to by a number of ancient historical sources, both Christian and non-Christian.

The primary source of information about the historical Jesus is the New Testament, which includes the Gospels of Matthew, Mark, Luke, and John. These texts were written in the decades following Jesus' death and are considered by scholars to be the earliest Christian texts. They provide accounts of Jesus' life, teachings, miracles, and death.

There are also several non-Christian historical sources that mention Jesus or provide information about the early Christian movement. Roman historians such as Tacitus, Suetonius and Pliny the Younger, as well as Jewish historian Flavius Josephus, all make reference to Jesus or early Christians. While these texts are not contemporary to Jesus' life and do not provide a detailed account of his life, they do attest to his historical existence.

Archaeological evidence also supports the historical existence of Jesus. For example, there is evidence that the city of Nazareth, where Jesus is said to have grown up, was a small village during the time when he would have lived. Additionally, there are several ancient inscriptions that reference Jesus or early Christians.

While the evidence of Jesus Christ existence is widely accepted by most historians, debates and skepticism still exist among scholars regarding the historical reliability of the Bible and other sources, and the extent of Jesus' divinity and miracles.

Did any of Jesus' contemporaries write about him?

There is no contemporary historical record of Jesus Christ that has been discovered so far. The earliest written accounts of Jesus come from the New Testament Gospels, which were written decades after his death. The New Testament gospels of Matthew, Mark, Luke, and John are considered to be the earliest Christian texts and provide accounts of Jesus' life, teachings, miracles, and death. The authors of these gospels are not known for certain, but they are traditionally attributed to Matthew, Mark, Luke, and John, who were said to be Jesus' disciples.

There are also several non-Christian historical sources that mention Jesus or provide information about the early Christian movement. Roman historians such as Tacitus, Suetonius, and Pliny the Younger, as well as Jewish historian Flavius Josephus, all make reference to Jesus or early Christians. These texts were written between 30-120 AD, a few decades after Jesus' death, but they do attest to his historical existence.

It is worth noting that the historical evidence for Jesus is limited and the lack of contemporary records does not necessarily mean Jesus did not exist. It is common for historical figures from this time period to lack contemporary records. Also, given that Jesus was a Jewish peasant who lived in a remote province of the Roman Empire and did not leave behind any writings himself, it is not surprising that there are not many historical records of him.

If Jesus existed, where are his descendants today?

If Jesus of Nazareth was a real historical person, it is possible that his descendants would still exist today, although it is impossible to determine with certainty.

According to the New Testament, Jesus was married to Mary Magdalene and had children with her. Some Christian traditions hold that Jesus had children and that his bloodline continues to

14

this day. However, this belief is not supported by any historical evidence and is not accepted by mainstream Christianity.

It is also worth noting that even if Jesus did have children, it is likely that his descendants would be very difficult to trace today. Many historical records from this time period have been lost and the lack of records would make it difficult to trace any descendants. Additionally, throughout history, many people have changed their names and moved around, making it difficult to trace descendants through genealogy.

In summary, it is possible that Jesus of Nazareth had descendants, but there is no evidence to support this and any descendants would be extremely difficult to trace today.

How would we go about determining if Jesus has descendants today?

Determining if Jesus of Nazareth had descendants and if any of them still exist today would be a complex and difficult task, as there is no historical evidence to support the existence of any descendants and many records from that time period have been lost. However, here are some possible ways that one could go about trying to determine if Jesus had descendants:

Genetic testing: If a living person claimed to be a descendant of Jesus, genetic testing could be used to determine if they were related. However, this would only be possible if a sample of Jesus' DNA was available for comparison, which is not the case.

Genealogical research: Genealogical research could be used to trace the lineage of Jesus' descendants, if they exist. However, this would be difficult due to the lack of records from that time period and the fact that many people have changed their names and moved around throughout history.

Historical research: Historical research could be used to search for any records or accounts from the time period that mention Jesus' descendants. However, as previously mentioned, there is no historical evidence to support the existence of any descendants.

DNA studies: DNA studies of people in areas where Jesus lived, such as the Middle East, could be used to search for genetic markers that might indicate a connection to Jesus. However, this is a controversial field and not accepted by many scientists.

It is important to note that even with the most advanced technology and scientific methods, it is highly unlikely to ever be able to conclusively prove or disprove the existence of Jesus' descendants.

Given the lack of historical evidence and the fact that it is not a widely accepted belief by the majority of scholars, the possibility of finding any descendants of Jesus today is highly unlikely.

When was the New Testament written?

The New Testament is a collection of texts that were written in the first century AD, primarily in the Greek language.

The exact dates of when the texts of the New Testament were written are not known with certainty, but they are generally believed to have been written between approximately 50-100 AD.

The Gospels of Matthew, Mark, Luke, and John, which provide accounts of the life, teachings, miracles, and death of Jesus, are believed to have been written between approximately 70-100 AD. They are considered to be the earliest Christian texts and form the core of the New Testament.

The letters of Paul, which form a large portion of the New Testament, are believed to have been written between approximately 50-65 AD. These letters, also called the "Pauline Epistles," were written by the apostle Paul and were addressed to early Christian communities.

The remaining texts of the New Testament, such as the letter of James, the letter of Peter, and the book of Revelation, are believed to have been written between approximately 50-100 AD.

It's worth noting that the dating of New Testament texts is based on scholarship and research, and there are different opinions among scholars about the exact dates of authorship.

How long after Jesus Christ died did the New Testament appear?

The New Testament texts were written several decades after the death of Jesus Christ, which is believed to have occurred around 30 AD.

The Gospel of Mark, which is believed to be the earliest of the four Gospels, is thought to have been written around 70 AD, which is approximately 40 years after Jesus' death. The Gospels of Matthew, Luke, and John are believed to have been written between 80-100 AD.

The letters of Paul, which form a large portion of the New Testament, are believed to have been written between 50-65 AD, which is between 20-35 years after Jesus' death.

The remaining texts of the New Testament, such as the letter of James, the letter of Peter, and the book of Revelation, are believed to have been written between 50-100 AD, which is between 20-70 years after Jesus' death.

It's worth noting that the dating of New Testament texts is based on scholarship and research, and there are different opinions among scholars about the exact dates of authorship. Some scholars suggest that some texts were written earlier than others, but a broad consensus places them within decades after Jesus' death.

What evidence is there that any of the Gospel writers knew Jesus?

There is no definitive historical evidence that any of the Gospel writers personally knew Jesus. The Gospels are a type of early Christian literature known as the "Synoptic Gospels," which means that they share a similar narrative and point of view. The authors of the Gospels, who are not named in the texts themselves, are traditionally believed to be Matthew, Mark, Luke, and John, but their identities are not certain. The texts were written decades after the death of Jesus, and it is likely that they are based on earlier oral traditions and written sources. Some scholars believe that the authors of the Gospels used these sources to compose their own accounts of Jesus' life and teachings, rather than writing from personal knowledge.

Where did the Gospel writers get information about Jesus' life?

The sources that the Gospel writers used to compose their accounts of Jesus' life and teachings are not certain, but scholars have proposed various theories.

One theory is that the authors of the Gospels used earlier oral traditions that had been passed down by word of mouth among the early Christian community. These traditions may have included stories about Jesus' life and teachings, as well as sayings attributed to him.

Another theory is that the authors of the Gospels used written sources, such as other Gospels or collections of Jesus' sayings, that were circulating among the early Christian community.

A further theory is that the authors of the Gospels were drawing from their own personal experiences and knowledge of the historical Jesus and his teachings.

It is also possible that the Gospel writers used a combination of these sources. The exact nature of the sources remains a subject of ongoing scholarly debate.

Who decided that we should believe in Jesus?

The belief in Jesus as a religious figure and the son of God, is a central tenet of Christianity. The origins of Christianity can be traced back to the first century CE in the region of Palestine, where Jesus lived and taught. The accounts of Jesus' life, teachings, and miracles are found in the New Testament Gospels, which were written by anonymous authors, who are traditionally believed to be Matthew, Mark, Luke, and John, decades after Jesus' death.

The early followers of Jesus, known as the apostles, began spreading his message and teachings, and Christianity gradually spread throughout the Roman Empire and beyond. The process of conversion and spreading the faith was not always peaceful, and there were many debates and controversies that took place among the early Christians.

The formation of the canon of the New Testament, which was the collection of texts that were deemed to be authoritative, was also a long process that took place over several centuries.

The belief in Jesus as the Son of God and the savior of humanity is a central tenet of Christianity, which is a monotheistic religion founded on the life, teachings, and death of Jesus of Nazareth. The belief in Jesus as the Messiah was first espoused by his followers, who were called early Christians, after his death and resurrection. They preached and spread their beliefs, leading to the formation of the Christian church. The belief in Jesus is based on the Bible, especially the New Testament which tells the story of Jesus's life, teachings and death and resurrection. The Bible is considered by Christians to be the word of God, and the belief in Jesus is considered to be a matter of faith.

It's important to note that Christianity is one of the world's major religions and its beliefs and practices have been passed down from generation to generation. Today, many people continue to believe in Jesus as the son of God, and the savior of humanity, based on their own personal faith, the testimony of others, and the reading and interpretation of the New Testament.

Where in the Bible does it say that Jesus was married?

The Bible does not state explicitly that Jesus was married. The New Testament, which is a collection of texts that tell the story of Jesus's life, teachings, and death, does not mention a wife or marriage for Jesus.

However, there are some texts that are not included in the New Testament, such as the "Gospel of Mary" and the "Gospel of Philip", that suggest Jesus had a close relationship with Mary Magdalene, and some scholars have argued that these texts imply that Jesus and Mary Magdalene were married. These texts are not considered to be part of the biblical canon by the majority of Christian denominations.

It's worth noting that in Christianity, Jesus is considered to be the son of God, the Messiah, and the savior of humanity, and the question of whether or not he was married is not central to the faith.

If there is no evidence that Jesus existed and the facts about his life cannot be verified, why do people still believe in Christ?

The question of whether Jesus existed and the veracity of the accounts of his life is a subject of ongoing scholarly debate. While there is no definitive historical evidence that Jesus existed, many scholars believe that he was a historical figure who lived in first-century Palestine and that the accounts of his life in the New

20

Testament Gospels are based on earlier oral and written traditions.

For many people, their belief in Jesus Christ is based on faith, which is the belief in something without the need for tangible evidence. Many Christians believe that Jesus is the Son of God and the savior of humanity, as stated in the New Testament, and that his teachings provide a path to salvation and eternal life. They believe that the message of Jesus, as well as the stories of his life, teachings, and miracles, have been passed down for centuries in the form of scripture and tradition, and that these teachings continue to hold relevance and meaning for people today.

Furthermore, Christianity has been around for over two thousand years and it has deeply influenced art, literature, culture, philosophy, politics, and social norms all over the world. The faith of Christianity has been passed down from generation to generation and it has developed an immense amount of traditions, practices, and rituals that shape the identity of millions of people.

Additionally, many people find comfort, guidance and personal fulfillment in the beliefs and practices of Christianity. They find that Christianity helps them understand their place in the world, gives them a sense of purpose and meaning, and provides a framework for how to live a good life.

In summary, while there is ongoing debate about the historical existence of Jesus and the veracity of the accounts of his life, many people continue to believe in Jesus Christ based on faith and the belief that his teachings provide a path to salvation and eternal life. Additionally, Christianity has had a significant impact on human history, culture and the personal lives of many people.

On Superbowl Sunday, do more people go to church or watch the Superbowl in the USA?

The Super Bowl is one of the most-watched television events in the United States, and it's likely that many people watch the game rather than going to church on Super Bowl Sunday. The Super Bowl is also considered a cultural phenomenon in the US and it's a day where family and friends gather together to watch the game, have parties, and enjoy the halftime show. That being said, church attendance can vary greatly depending on location, denomination, and the time of the service. Some churches may choose to hold special or alternative services on Super Bowl Sunday to accommodate those who want to attend church before or after the game. Some churches may also have events or activities that are related to the Super Bowl or have special messages related to the game.

Are Gods more important to rich people or poor people?

The importance of gods to rich people and poor people is a topic that is open to interpretation and can vary greatly depending on the culture, religion, and belief system in question.

In some cases, people living in poverty may find solace and comfort in their belief in gods, as they may see them as a source of hope, protection and guidance in difficult times. Similarly, people living in poverty may see their belief in gods as a way of making sense of their difficult circumstances and as a way of finding meaning in their suffering.

On the other hand, some wealthy people may also find comfort and guidance in their belief in gods, and may see them as a source of inspiration, wisdom, and spiritual fulfillment. They may also seek the guidance of gods in their decision-making, and may see them as a source of moral and ethical guidance.

It's important to note that the concept of God and the belief in their existence is a complex and multifaceted topic that varies greatly depending on the culture, religion and belief system in question, and people's beliefs on this topic are often deeply personal, and are influenced by many factors, such as culture, upbringing, education and personal experiences.

If every human being were healthy, rich and powerful, would we still need Gods?

The question of whether or not humans would still need gods if they were healthy, rich and powerful is a complex topic that is open to interpretation. Some argue that the need for gods is rooted in the human condition, which includes the fear of death, the desire for security, and the need for meaning and purpose in life. Therefore, if humans were healthy, rich and powerful, they may not feel the same need for gods to provide them with protection and guidance.

Others argue that the belief in gods is not solely based on practical needs, but is also a reflection of deeper spiritual and existential questions about the meaning and purpose of life. Even if humans were to achieve perfect health, wealth, and power, they may still seek something beyond the material world, and gods may continue to serve as a source of inspiration, guidance, and spiritual fulfillment.

Additionally, in certain cultures, religions and belief systems, gods are not seen as providers of material things, but as spiritual entities, the belief in them is not based on the need of material things.

It's important to note that the concept of God and the belief in their existence is a complex and multifaceted topic that varies greatly depending on the religion or belief system in question, and people's beliefs on this topic are often deeply personal, and are influenced by many factors, such as culture, upbringing, education and personal experiences.

Do animals believe in Gods?

The question of whether animals believe in gods is a topic that is open to interpretation and is difficult to answer with certainty. While it is true that many animals have complex cognitive abilities and can exhibit behaviors that are consistent with certain forms of religious or spiritual beliefs, it is not possible to know for sure if animals hold the same concept of gods that humans do.

Animals do not have the capacity for abstract reasoning, and they can't communicate their beliefs in the same way that humans can. Therefore, it is not possible to know if animals believe in gods or not.

It's important to note that the concept of God and the belief in their existence is a complex and multifaceted topic that varies greatly depending on the culture, religion and belief system in question, and it is based on human understanding and interpretation. Additionally, this question is based on assumptions and hypotheses and it is not possible to provide a factual answer as it is not possible to prove or disprove the existence of gods and their relation with animals.

What would happen to the Gods if humans go extinct?

The question of what would happen to the gods if humans were to go extinct is a topic of much debate and speculation among theologians and philosophers.

One perspective is that gods are not dependent on human belief or worship for their existence, and therefore, if humans were to go extinct, the gods would continue to exist regardless. In this view, gods are seen as eternal and unchanging entities that exist independently of the human race.

Another perspective is that gods are a product of human imagination and belief, and therefore, if humans were to go extinct, the gods would also cease to exist. In this view, gods are seen as symbolic representations of natural forces and human emotions, and are not independent entities.

It's important to note that the concept of God and the belief in their existence is a complex and multifaceted topic that varies greatly depending on the culture, religion, and belief system in question. Additionally, this question is based on assumptions and hypotheses and it is not possible to provide a factual answer as it is not possible to prove or disprove the existence of gods and their relation with humans.

Who are the most influential human beings to have ever lived?

The question of the most influential human beings to have ever lived are is a matter of opinion, and different people may have different views on who should be considered "great." It is also important to consider that different cultures and time periods may have different perspectives on what makes someone great.

However, throughout history, there have been many individuals who have made significant contributions to their fields and have left a lasting impact on the world. Some examples include.

Alexander the Great, who conquered much of the known world and spread Greek culture and ideas.

Isaac Newton, who made important contributions to physics, mathematics, and astronomy, and laid the foundation for modern science.

Mahatma Gandhi, who led India to independence through non-violent civil disobedience.

Martin Luther King Jr., who played a key role in the Civil Rights Movement and helped to end segregation in the United States.

Marie Curie, who was the first woman to win a Nobel Prize and made important contributions to the field of physics and chemistry.

Nelson Mandela, who helped to end apartheid in South Africa and served as the country's first black president.

Albert Einstein, who made groundbreaking contributions to the field of physics and developed the theory of general relativity.

William Shakespeare, who is widely considered one of the greatest writers in the English language, and whose plays are still performed and read all over the world.

Leonardo da Vinci, who was a polymath and made important contributions to fields such as art, science, and engineering.

Socrates, who is considered one of the founders of Western philosophy, and is known for his Socratic method of teaching.

It's worth noting that this is just a small selection of examples, and there are many other individuals throughout history who have made significant contributions and have left a lasting impact on the world.

Who is the single greatest human being to have ever lived?

It's a matter of opinion who is the single greatest human being to have ever lived, as different people may have different views on who should be considered the "greatest." It's also important to consider that different cultures and time periods may have different perspectives on what makes someone great.

It's difficult to pick one person from all of human history as the "greatest" as it depends on what criteria one uses to evaluate greatness. Some may argue that it is a religious figure, like Jesus, Buddha, or Muhammad, for the spiritual guidance they provided and the impact they had on their respective religions. Others might argue it's a political leader such as Abraham Lincoln or Martin Luther King Jr. for the impact they had on their respective countries. Still, others might argue it's a scientist like Isaac Newton or Albert Einstein, or an artist like Leonardo da Vinci or Shakespeare, for their contributions to human knowledge and culture.

It's important to remember that greatness is a subjective term and it can be influenced by many factors such as personal values, cultural background, and historical context. It's a complex and multi-faceted concept that can't be reduced to a single person or a simple answer.

Who are the most influential humans ever?

It's difficult to compile a definitive list of the most influential humans ever, as it would depend on one's perspective and criteria for "influence." However, here are some notable figures from history that have had a significant impact on the world:

Jesus Christ
Muhammad
Confucius
Buddah
Julius Caesar
Alexander the Great
Napoleon Bonaparte
Abraham Lincoln
Mahatma Gandhi
Martin Luther King Jr.
Isaac Newton
Galileo Galilei
Charles Darwin
Albert Einstein
Leonardo da Vinci

Michelangelo
William Shakespeare
Johann Sebastian Bach
Wolfgang Amadeus Mozart
Ludwig van Beethoven
George Washington
Abraham Lincoln

This list is not exhaustive, there are many other influential people throughout history, and it could be different based on different regions and cultures. Also, it's important to note that influence can be positive or negative, it's not just about the impact on the world but how it was perceived.

Who are the most villainous humans ever?

It's difficult to compile a definitive list of the most villainous humans ever, as it would depend on one's perspective and criteria for "villainous." However, here are some notable figures from history that have committed heinous acts and have had a significant negative impact on the world:

Adolf Hitler
Joseph Stalin
Mao Zedong
Pol Pot
Kim Jong-un
Osama bin Laden
Genghis Khan
Emperor Hirohito
Emperor Nero
Emperor Caligula
Emperor Commodus
Emperor Maximinus Thrax
Emperor Caracalla
Emperor Alexander Sererus
Emperor Valerian
Emperor Diocletian

Emperor Constantine 1
Emperor Constantine 2
Emperor Julian
Emperor Jovian

It's important to note that influence can be positive or negative, it's not just about the impact on the world but how it was perceived. This list is not exhaustive, there are many other villainous people throughout history, and it could be different based on different regions and cultures. Also, this list is composed of historical figures who had a significant negative impact on the world, through war, genocide, human rights violations, and other atrocities.

What is the history of humanity and its major achievements?

Human history is a long and complex subject that spans thousands of years and covers many different cultures and civilizations. Some of the major achievements of humanity include:

The development of agriculture, which allowed for the settled existence of human communities and the growth of civilization.

The invention of writing, which allowed for the recording of history, the creation of literature, and the spread of knowledge.

The creation of complex societies and governments, including the ancient empires of Egypt, China, and Rome.

The scientific revolution and the subsequent development of modern science, which has led to a greater understanding of the natural world and technological advancements.

The industrial revolution, which led to the widespread use of machines in manufacturing and the growth of large-scale industry.

The development of democracy and human rights, which have led to greater freedom and equality for many people around the world.

This list is not exhaustive, there are many other achievements of humanity, such as the creation of art, music and literature, the development of medicine and healthcare, and the creation of new technologies like the computer and internet.

Where did humans come from?

Humans evolved from primates, specifically from a group of apes called hominids. This process of evolution took place over millions of years and is supported by a significant amount of scientific evidence, including the study of fossils, DNA, and comparative anatomy. The earliest known human ancestor is believed to be a species called Australopithecus afarensis, which lived around 3-4 million years ago in Africa. Over time, various human-like species developed, including Homo habilis, Homo erectus, and finally Homo sapiens, the species to which modern humans belong.

Is Africa or Asia the cradle of civilization?

The term "cradle of civilization" is often used to refer to the regions of the world where civilization first emerged. The Fertile Crescent, which includes present-day Iraq, Syria, Lebanon, Israel, and parts of Turkey and Egypt, is often considered the birthplace of civilization. However, the earliest civilizations also emerged independently in other parts of the world, including ancient China, India, and Africa, such as ancient Egypt.

What is it that allowed humans to become so intelligent?

The evolution of human intelligence is a complex and multi-faceted process that is still not fully understood. However, scientists have proposed several key factors that may have contributed to the development of human intelligence.

One important factor is the development of the human brain, which is much larger and more complex than the brains of other primates. This allowed for the evolution of advanced cognitive abilities, such as the ability to think abstractly, use language, and plan for the future.

Another important factor is the development of tools and technology, which allowed early humans to exploit new resources and adapt to new environments. This in turn led to the evolution of skills such as problem-solving, innovation, and planning.

Social and cultural factors also played a role in the evolution of human intelligence. Humans have developed complex societies and cultures, which have led to the development of shared knowledge, norms and values. This allowed human ancestors to learn from one another and pass down knowledge and skills from generation to generation.

Lastly, the evolution of human intelligence may also have been driven by selective pressures, such as the need to outcompete other species for resources or to defend oneself from predators.

Due to our intelligence, are humans an accident or a mistake?

It is not accurate to say that humans are an accident or a mistake. Evolution is a natural process that does not have a specific goal or purpose. It is driven by random genetic mutations and natural selection, which together lead to the development of new species over time.

Humans are the result of millions of years of evolution. Our ancestors faced various challenges and pressures, and those that were better able to adapt and survive passed on their genetic traits to the next generation. The development of human intelligence is one of the characteristics that allowed our ancestors to survive and thrive in their environment.

It's important to understand that evolution doesn't have any moral or ethical values, it doesn't have good or bad outcomes. Evolution is a neutral process, it's simply a way of describing how the natural world changes over time.

It's also important to note that human intelligence is not the only measure of worth or value of a species, it's just one characteristic among many. The diversity of life on Earth is a precious and valuable thing, and all species play a role in maintaining the delicate balance of the ecosystem.

What is the most widely accepted scientific explanation for how the universe was created?

The scientific explanation for the origin of the universe is the Big Bang theory. The Big Bang theory states that the universe began as a singularity, an infinitely hot and dense point in space-time, around 13.8 billion years ago. This singularity expanded and cooled, leading to the formation of subatomic particles, and eventually atoms. As the universe continued to expand and cool, matter began to clump together under the influence of gravity, forming stars and galaxies.

The Big Bang theory is supported by a great deal of observational evidence, such as the cosmic microwave background radiation, which is thought to be the residual heat left over from the Big Bang, and the observed large-scale structure of the universe. The theory also predicts the relative abundance of the light elements, such as hydrogen and helium, which have been observed to match the predictions of the Big Bang to a high degree of accuracy.

It's worth mentioning that the Big Bang theory is not a complete explanation of the origin of the universe, it only describes the origin and evolution of the observable universe, and it doesn't explain what caused the singularity or what existed before it. Some theories such as the Inflationary cosmology, try to provide answers to these questions.

What are the different theories explaining the creation of the universe?

There are several different theories that attempt to explain the creation of the universe, but the most widely accepted among scientists is the Big Bang theory.

The Big Bang theory states that the universe began as a singularity, an infinitely hot and dense point in space-time, around 13.8 billion years ago. This singularity expanded and cooled, leading to the formation of subatomic particles, and eventually atoms. As the universe continued to expand and cool, matter began to clump together under the influence of gravity, forming stars and galaxies.

Another popular theory is the steady state theory, which posits that the universe has always existed and is constantly creating new matter to form new galaxies, so that the average properties of the universe remain constant over time. However, it has been largely discredited because it could not explain the observed cosmic microwave background radiation and the large scale structure of the universe.

A third theory is the oscillating universe theory, which suggests that the universe goes through an infinite series of cycles, each beginning with a Big Bang and ending with a Big Crunch, a collapse of the universe that eventually leads to another Big Bang. But it also has been largely discarded, as it does not explain why the universe is accelerating in its expansion.

Finally, there are also theories that propose that the universe is a simulation, or that it exists within a higher-dimensional space, or that it is one of many universes within a multiverse. These theories are still speculative and lack observational evidence.

How can the universe come from nothing?

The idea that the universe could come from "nothing" is a topic of ongoing debate and research in physics and cosmology. One popular explanation is the idea of quantum fluctuations, which suggest that energy can fluctuate in and out of existence in a vacuum, a region of space that is empty of matter. These fluctuations can result in the creation of subatomic particles, which can then combine to form atoms and eventually stars and galaxies.

Another explanation is the concept of "virtual particles," which are subatomic particles that can spontaneously come into existence and then annihilate each other in a very short period of time. These particles can also be thought of as fluctuations in the energy of the vacuum

Additionally, theories such as inflationary cosmology, propose that the universe began as a tiny patch of space-time that rapidly expanded in a process known as inflation, and that this expansion was driven by a form of energy that existed in the vacuum.

It's worth noting that while these theories suggest that something can come from "nothing," they do not explain the ultimate cause or origin of the universe. They only provide explanations for the beginning of our observable universe.

In any case, the question of how the universe can come from "nothing" is still an open question in physics and cosmology, and it is an active area of research that scientists are still trying to understand.

What is the universe made of?

The universe is made up of a variety of different types of matter and energy. The majority of the universe is made up of dark matter and dark energy, which cannot be directly observed but can be inferred through their gravitational effects on visible matter. About 4% of the universe is made up of "normal" matter, which is the type of matter that makes up stars, planets, and galaxies. This normal matter is made up of protons, neutrons, and electrons. About 73% of the universe is made up of dark energy, a mysterious form of energy that is causing the expansion of the universe to accelerate. The remaining 23% is made up of dark matter, a mysterious form of matter that does not interact with light or other forms of electromagnetic radiation, but can be inferred through its gravitational effects on visible matter.

How was our solar system created?

Our solar system was created about 4.6 billion years ago from a giant cloud of gas and dust, known as the solar nebula. The cloud began to collapse under its own gravity, and as it did, it began to spin. As the cloud collapsed, it grew denser and hotter in the center, eventually forming the sun. The remaining material flattened into a spinning disc, from which the planets and other bodies in the solar system formed through a process known as accretion. This process involved small particles sticking together to form larger ones, which then stuck together to form even larger ones, and so on, until eventually the planets and other bodies we see today were formed.

How was the Earth created?

The Earth was created about 4.5 billion years ago, as part of the process of forming the solar system. As a cloud of gas and dust, known as the solar nebula, collapsed under its own gravity, it formed a spinning disc of material. In the center of this disc, the sun formed, while the remaining material flattened into a spinning disc, from which the planets and other bodies in the solar system formed through a process known as accretion. This process involved small particles sticking together to form larger ones, which then stuck together to form even larger ones, and so on, until eventually the planets and other bodies we see today were formed.

The Earth formed from the dust and gas that remained in the inner solar system, where temperatures were too high for volatile materials like water and methane to condense. As dust and rock accreted, they collided and stuck together, gradually forming larger and larger objects called planetesimals. Over time, these planetesimals collided and merged to form the Earth and the other inner planets. The heat generated by these collisions caused the early Earth to melt, creating a magma ocean. As the planet cooled, a solid crust formed on its surface and the first oceans formed. This process is known as planetary accretion.

How did life begin on Earth?

The origin of life on Earth is a topic of ongoing research and debate among scientists. There are several different theories about how life may have first originated, but no single theory has yet been proven.

One of the most widely accepted theories is that life began through a process called abiogenesis, which refers to the origin of life from non-living matter. This process is thought to have occurred in the Earth's oceans around 4 billion years ago. The first living organisms were simple, single-celled organisms, such as bacteria, that existed in a "primordial soup" of organic molecules. These molecules, including amino acids, nucleotides and lipids, could have been produced through natural processes such as lightning, volcanic activity, and radiation.

Another theory is that life on Earth came from an extraterrestrial source, such as comets or meteorites that delivered the building blocks of life to Earth, this is called Panspermia.

The precise details of how life first originated on Earth are still not fully understood, and further research is needed to fully understand the processes that led to the emergence of life on our planet.

What did all life on Earth evolve from?

All life on Earth is thought to have evolved from a common ancestor, through a process called evolution by natural selection. This process is driven by genetic variation, which occurs through mutations in the genetic material of organisms. These mutations can then be passed on to the next generation, and if they confer an advantage to the organism in its environment, it is more likely to survive and reproduce, passing the advantageous mutation on to its offspring. Over time, this process can lead to the development of new species, as populations of organisms diverge and become reproductively isolated from one another.

The first living organisms on Earth were simple, single-celled organisms, such as bacteria, that existed around 4 billion years ago. Over time, these simple organisms evolved and diversified, eventually giving rise to more complex forms of life, such as multicellular organisms. All living organisms on Earth today, from the simplest bacteria to the most complex mammals, are thought to have evolved from a common ancestor, through a process of descent with modification.

Why can organisms not live forever?

Organisms cannot live forever because of the accumulation of damage to their cells and DNA over time. The process of living, such as metabolism, generates harmful byproducts, like free radicals, that can damage cells and DNA. Additionally, environmental factors such as UV radiation, toxins, and pathogens can also cause damage to cells and DNA.

Cells are also constantly dividing, which can lead to errors in the replication of DNA, creating mutations. Over time, these mutations can accumulate and cause cells to malfunction and eventually leading to the death of the organism.

Also, organisms have a limited number of cell divisions due to the presence of telomeres, which are the protective caps on the ends of chromosomes. Each time a cell divides, the telomeres shorten, and when they become too short, the cell can no longer divide, leading to cell death.

All these factors contribute to the aging process and ultimately leads to the death of the organism. Some organisms have evolved mechanisms to delay the aging process, such as calorie restriction, but they too cannot live forever.

In summary, organisms cannot live forever due to the accumulation of damage to their cells and DNA over time, and the eventual failure of systems that maintain the integrity of cells and DNA.

How many mass extinction events have occurred on Earth?

There have been several mass extinction events throughout the history of Earth, in which large numbers of species became extinct in a relatively short period of time. The most well-known mass extinction event is the one that occurred at the end of the Cretaceous period, around 65 million years ago, which wiped out the dinosaurs and many other species.

The exact number of mass extinction events that have occurred on Earth is a topic of ongoing research, but scientists generally agree that there have been at least five major mass extinction events in the Earth's history, often referred to as the "big five" mass extinctions.

The End-Ordovician extinction, around 443 million years ago, which wiped out around 85% of marine species.

The Late Devonian extinction, around 374 million years ago, which killed off around 75% of all species.

The End-Permian extinction, around 252 million years ago, which is considered the largest mass extinction event in Earth's history, wiping out around 96% of all marine species and 70% of terrestrial species.

The End-Triassic extinction, around 201 million years ago, which killed off around 80% of all species.

The End-Cretaceous extinction, around 65 million years ago, which wiped out the dinosaurs and many other species

In addition to these five major mass extinction events, there have been several smaller mass extinction events throughout Earth's history. Scientists continue to study these events to understand the causes and consequences of mass extinctions.

Is global warming a new phenomenon?

Global warming, or the gradual increase in the average temperature of the Earth's surface, is not a new phenomenon. The Earth's climate has naturally varied throughout its history due to a variety of factors, such as changes in the Earth's orbit, volcanic activity, and variations in solar radiation. However, the current global warming trend is different from these natural fluctuations in that it is largely caused by human activities, particularly the burning of fossil fuels which releases greenhouse gases such as carbon dioxide and methane into the atmosphere, which traps heat and causes the Earth's temperature to rise.

The current warming trend is considered unusual in the context of the past 2,000 years, with the 20th century being the warmest century in the last 1,500 years. Since the preindustrial era, the average global temperature has risen by around 1.1 degrees Celsius (2 degrees Fahrenheit) with more than two thirds of that warming has occurred since 1980. This warming trend is projected to continue in the future if greenhouse gas emissions are not reduced.

In summary, global warming is not a new phenomenon, however the current warming trend is unusual in the context of the past 2,000 years, and is primarily caused by human activities, particularly the burning of fossil fuels.

What happens during a global warming event?

Global warming can lead to a variety of impacts on the Earth's climate and ecosystems. Some of the most significant impacts include:

Rising sea levels: As the Earth's temperature increases, the polar ice caps melt and glaciers retreat, causing the sea level to rise. This can lead to coastal flooding and erosion, and can also have significant impacts on island nations and low-lying areas.

Increased frequency and severity of extreme weather events: Global warming can lead to an increase in the frequency and severity of extreme weather events, such as heat waves, droughts, and heavy precipitation. This can have significant impacts on agriculture, water resources, and human health.

Changes in precipitation patterns: Global warming can lead to changes in precipitation patterns, with some areas experiencing more frequent and severe droughts, while others experience increased flooding.

Ocean acidification: As the ocean absorbs carbon dioxide, it becomes more acidic, which can have significant impacts on marine life, including coral reefs, shellfish, and other organisms that rely on calcium carbonate to build their shells or skeletons.

Impact on biodiversity: Global warming can lead to changes in the distribution and abundance of species, as well as changes in the timing of seasonal events such as migration, reproduction and blooming. This can result in the loss of biodiversity, ecosystem degradation and collapse.

Impact on human health: Global warming can lead to heat-related illnesses and deaths, increased air pollution, increased spread of disease through insects and pests, and food and water shortages.

These impacts are not limited to one region or sector, they are interrelated and they can exacerbate each other. Some of the impacts of global warming can be mitigated by reducing greenhouse gas emissions and implementing adaptation measures.

Do Ice Ages follow global warming events?

Ice ages, or periods of long-term cooling and glacial expansion, are not directly caused by global warming. The Earth's climate is influenced by a complex set of factors, including changes in the Earth's orbit, variations in solar radiation, and volcanic activity. The current warming trend, caused primarily by human activities, such as the burning of fossil fuels which releases greenhouse gases into the atmosphere, is not directly causing an ice age.

The Earth has experienced several ice ages throughout its history, with the most recent one ending around 11,700 years ago. These ice ages were caused by a combination of factors, including changes in the Earth's orbit and variations in solar radiation, and are not directly related to the current warming trend.

It's important to note that the term "ice age" is often used to describe a specific period of Earth's history when ice sheets covered large parts of the planet and the global temperature was much colder than today. However, the Earth's climate is always changing and currently we are in a interglacial period, which is a warmer period within an ice age.

In summary, Ice ages are not directly caused by global warming, but rather by a complex set of factors including changes in the Earth's orbit, variations in solar radiation, and volcanic activity. The current warming trend caused by human activities is not directly causing an ice age.

How long have humans been on Earth?

Humans, or Homo sapiens, have been on Earth for around 200,000 years. The first anatomically modern humans (AMH) are believed to have appeared around 200,000 years ago in Africa, and over time, they spread out of Africa and colonized other parts of the world.

The earliest known anatomically modern human fossils were found in the Omo Kibish Formation in southern Ethiopia, and are dated to around 195,000-160,000 years ago. The oldest known fossils of Homo sapiens outside of Africa were found in the Misliya Cave in Israel and are dated around 177,000-194,000 years old.

The exact timing and process of the emergence of anatomically modern humans is still a topic of ongoing research and debate among scientists, but there is general agreement that the first anatomically modern humans appeared in Africa around 200,000 years ago and spread around the world over time.

It's important to note that while anatomically modern humans have been around for around 200,000 years, the development of human culture, civilization and technology has occurred much more recently. The emergence of agriculture, urbanization, and written language are some examples of the cultural and technological advancements that have occurred only in the last 10,000 years or so.

What are the negative impacts of humans on Earth?

Humans have had a significant impact on the Earth and its ecosystems. Some of the most significant impacts include:

Habitat destruction and loss of biodiversity: Human activities such as deforestation, urbanization, and agriculture have led to the destruction of natural habitats and the loss of biodiversity. Many species have gone extinct or are endangered as a result of human activities.

Climate change: Human activities, particularly the burning of fossil fuels, have led to an increase in the concentration of greenhouse gases in the atmosphere, causing the Earth's temperature to rise and leading to climate change.

Pollution: Human activities have led to the pollution of the air, water, and soil with chemicals and other toxins, which can have harmful impacts on human health and the environment.

Overexploitation of natural resources: Human populations have grown rapidly in recent history, and as a result, natural resources such as fresh water, forests, and fisheries have been overexploited, leading to their depletion.

Soil degradation: Human activities such as agriculture, urbanization, and deforestation have led to the degradation of soil quality, reducing its productivity and ability to support plant and animal life.

Ocean acidification: As the ocean absorbs carbon dioxide, it becomes more acidic, which can have significant impacts on marine life, including coral reefs, shellfish, and other organisms that rely on calcium carbonate to build their shells or skeletons.

Spread of invasive species: Human activities have led to the unintentional or deliberate introduction of non-native species into new areas, which can outcompete or prey on native species, leading to declines in biodiversity

All these impacts are interrelated and they can exacerbate each other. It's important to note that many of these impacts can be mitigated by reducing human activities that are harmful to the environment, and implementing conservation and sustainable development practices.

What positive impacts have humans had on the Earth?

Humans have had a complex relationship with the Earth and its ecosystems, and while many of our impacts have been negative, we have also had some positive impacts. Some examples include:

Advances in medicine and healthcare: Humans have developed a wide range of medical treatments and technologies that have greatly improved human health and longevity.

Improvements in food production: Humans have developed a wide range of agricultural techniques and technologies that have greatly increased food production, helping to feed a growing global population.

Advances in technology: Humans have developed a wide range of technologies that have greatly improved our ability to understand and interact with the world around us, and have also led to many other positive developments such as clean energy, efficient transportation, and communication systems.

Conservation efforts: Humans have also put effort to preserve and protect the environment. Through conservation and preservation efforts, many species have been saved from extinction, and many habitats and ecosystems have been protected and restored.

Environmental regulations: Governments around the world have implemented laws and regulations to protect the environment, such as clean air and water acts, and regulations on pollution and waste disposal.

Sustainable development: Many communities and organizations are implementing sustainable development practices, which aim to balance economic development with the protection of the environment and social well-being.

Climate action: The global community has taken steps to address climate change through the United Nations Framework Convention on Climate Change and the Paris Agreement, which aim to reduce greenhouse gas emissions and mitigate the impacts of climate change.

It's important to note that these positive impacts are also interrelated and can be further enhanced by continuing research, development and implementation of sustainable practices.

What are some secret organizations that have existed throughout history?

Throughout history, there have been many secret organizations that have existed for various reasons, such as political, religious, or ideological purposes. Some examples include:

Freemasons: A fraternal organization that traces its origins to the local fraternities of stonemasons, which from the end of the fourteenth century regulated the qualifications of stonemasons and their interaction with authorities and clients.

Illuminati: A secret society founded in Bavaria in the late 1700s that sought to influence political decisions and promote rationalism and free thought.

Rosicrucians: A secret society that emerged in the early 1600s and was associated with the spread of Hermeticism and alchemy.

Knights Templar: A medieval Christian military order that was founded in the 12th century to protect Christian pilgrims in the Holy Land.

Bilderberg Group: A secretive annual invitation-only conference established in 1954, comprising around 130-140 political leaders and experts from industry, finance, academia, and the media.

Bohemian Club: A private club with some notable members, which is known for its annual gathering of some of the most powerful men in the world at Bohemian Grove, a 2,700-acre campground in Monte Rio, California.

Triads: Secret societies, primarily based in the Greater China area, that have been involved in organized crime, drug trafficking, and money laundering.

Skull and Bones: A secret society at Yale University in New Haven, Connecticut. It is one of the oldest and most famous of the college societies in the United States.

These are just a few examples of secret organizations that have existed throughout history, and there are many more. It's important to note that the existence and activities of these organizations are often shrouded in secrecy and speculation, making it difficult to know the full extent of their influence or activities.

Which secret organizations are still active today?

Many of the secret organizations that have existed throughout history are no longer active, or their activities are significantly diminished. However, some organizations that were founded in the past are still active today, although the extent of their influence and activities is often difficult to determine.

Some examples of secret organizations that are thought to be active today include:

Freemasons: Freemasonry is still active today, with members in many countries around the world. They are known to have charitable activities and rituals, which are kept secret among its members.

Illuminati: While the original Illuminati organization was disbanded in the late 1700s, various groups and individuals have claimed to be associated with the Illuminati in modern times. However, there is no evidence that any of these groups have the same level of influence or power as the original Illuminati.

Triads: Triads are still active today, especially in Southeast Asia, where they are involved in organized crime, drug trafficking, and money laundering.

Bilderberg Group: The Bilderberg Group still holds an annual conference, bringing together around 130-140 political leaders and experts from industry, finance, academia, and the media, but the activities and discussions are kept secret.

Some Secret Societies in Universities: Some secret societies in universities, such as Skull and Bones at Yale University, are still active today, but their activities are not public.

It is important to note that the existence and activities of these organizations are often shrouded in secrecy, and information about their activities is often difficult to verify.

What species of animals have humans caused to go extinct?

Humans have been responsible for the extinction of many species of animals throughout history. Some examples include:

The dodo, a flightless bird native to the island of Mauritius, which was hunted to extinction by sailors and settlers in the 17th century.

The passenger pigeon, once one of the most abundant bird species in North America, which was hunted to extinction in the late 19th century.

The great auk, a flightless bird that lived in the North Atlantic, which was hunted to extinction in the 19th century.

The quagga, a subspecies of the plains zebra, which was hunted to extinction in the late 19th century.

The woolly mammoth, which lived in the Arctic regions of the Northern Hemisphere, went extinct around 4,000 years ago.

The saber-toothed tiger, that lived in North and South America, went extinct around 11,000 years ago.

The Steller's sea cow, a large marine mammal that lived in the Bering Sea, which was hunted to extinction in the 18th century.

The Tasmanian tiger, a marsupial native to Tasmania, which was hunted to extinction in the 20th century.

What are the positive and negative impacts of globalization?

Positive impacts of globalization include increased economic growth and development, access to a wider variety of goods and services, and the ability for people to communicate and share ideas with others around the world. Negative impacts of globalization include loss of jobs and industries in developed countries, cultural homogenization, and increased income inequality. Additionally, globalization can lead to negative environmental effects, as increased trade and transportation can contribute to climate change.

What is the impact of globalization on the spread of diseases?

Globalization can have a significant impact on the spread of diseases. The increased movement of people, goods, and animals across borders can facilitate the rapid spread of infectious diseases. For example, the outbreak of COVID-19 in Wuhan, China in 2019 quickly spread to other countries via international travel, leading to a global pandemic.

Additionally, globalization can contribute to the emergence and reemergence of diseases. The increased trade in wild animals and the destruction of natural habitats can bring humans into contact with new pathogens. The intensification of livestock production and the global trade in live animals also increases the risk of disease spread. Climate change, another consequence of globalization, also plays a role in the emergence of new diseases by altering the distribution of vectors and pathogens.

On the other hand, globalization can also have positive effects on disease control and public health. Advances in transportation and communication have made it easier to respond to disease outbreaks and to share information and resources between countries. Additionally, international trade and investment can support economic development, which can improve living standards and health outcomes.

In summary, globalization can have both positive and negative impacts on the spread of diseases, depending on the specific context.

What forms of transportation spreads diseases the most?

Air travel is one of the main forms of transportation that can spread diseases. Airplanes can transport infected individuals to new locations, allowing diseases to spread quickly to other countries and continents. The close quarters of an airplane cabin can also facilitate the spread of infectious diseases through the air or through contact with contaminated surfaces. Additionally, the high volume of international travelers can make it difficult to track and contain outbreaks.

Other forms of transportation that can contribute to the spread of diseases include trains, buses, and ships. These forms of transportation can also transport infected individuals to new locations, and can also facilitate the spread of disease through close contact with other passengers.

However, it's worth noting that transportation is not the only factor that contributes to the spread of diseases, and it can interact with other factors such as population density, human behavior, and existing health systems.

What are the positive and negative impacts of stock markets on humans?

Positive impacts of stock markets on humans include:

Economic growth: Stock markets can provide a significant source of funding for businesses and entrepreneurs, which can lead to increased economic activity and job creation.

Investment opportunities: Stock markets give individuals and institutions the ability to invest in a wide variety of companies, which can provide a potential for higher returns than other investments. This can help people to achieve their financial goals and improve their standard of living.

Consumer benefit: Companies that are publicly traded on stock markets may be more accountable to their shareholders and more likely to focus on producing quality goods and services

47

at competitive prices. This can lead to better products and services for consumers.

Retirement savings: Stock markets can provide a way for people to save for retirement through investment in stocks, mutual funds, and other securities.

Negative impacts of stock markets on humans include:

Volatility: Stock markets can be highly volatile and subject to sudden and dramatic changes in value. This can lead to significant losses for individual investors and can cause people to lose their savings.

Income inequality: Stock markets can benefit those who have the resources to invest, while having little impact on those without such resources, thus increasing income inequality.

Short-term focus: Companies may prioritize short-term financial performance over long-term sustainability in order to meet the expectations of stock market investors, which can negatively impact the economy and society as a whole.

Psychological impact: The volatility of stock markets can lead to psychological distress for investors who are heavily invested in stocks. This can include feelings of anxiety, fear, and depression.

Speculation: Stock markets can be subject to speculation and manipulation, which can lead to artificial price inflation and instability. This can create uncertainty and can negatively impact the economy and society.

Overall, stock markets can provide significant benefits to humans, but they also come with risks and potential downsides. It's important for individuals to carefully consider their investment strategies and to be aware of the potential risks and benefits associated with stock market investing.

What are the positive and negative impacts of stock markets on the Earth?

Positive impacts of stock markets on the Earth include:

48

Environmental friendly investments: Stock markets can provide opportunities for investors to support companies and projects that promote sustainability and environmental stewardship.

Green finance: Stock markets can provide a source of funding for renewable energy projects, sustainable transportation, and other green initiatives, which can help to reduce greenhouse gas emissions and mitigate the effects of climate change.

Negative impacts of stock markets on the Earth include:

Environmental degradation: Companies may prioritize short-term financial performance over long-term environmental sustainability in order to meet the expectations of stock market investors, which can lead to environmental degradation and pollution.

Carbon emissions: Companies that are publicly traded on stock markets may not have incentives to reduce carbon emissions, as they may prioritize their profits over the environment.

Natural resource exploitation: Stock markets can provide funding for extractive industries such as oil and gas, mining, and logging, which can lead to the destruction of natural habitats and the depletion of natural resources.

Climate risks: Climate change can also lead to financial risks for stock markets, as it can cause physical damage to assets and disrupt supply chains.

Overall, stock markets can provide opportunities for investment in environmentally friendly initiatives, but they also come with risks and potential downsides. It's important for investors to carefully consider the environmental impact of their investments and to be aware of the potential risks and benefits associated with stock market investing.

Should stock markets be eliminated?

Stock markets play an important role in the global economy by providing a source of funding for companies and offering investment opportunities for individuals and institutions. Eliminating stock markets would likely have significant negative consequences for economic growth and development.

However, it's important to consider ways to improve the functioning of stock markets and address the negative impacts that they can have. Some possible solutions include:

Regulating markets to prevent speculation and manipulation

Encouraging long-term investment and sustainability-oriented investing

Increasing transparency and accountability for companies listed on stock markets

Promoting more responsible and environmentally-friendly business practices

Encouraging the growth of alternative forms of financing such as crowdfunding and community investment

In summary, stock markets provide many benefits to the economy and society, but it's important to address the negative impacts they can have and to explore ways to improve their functioning. Eliminating stock markets altogether is not necessary and would have many negative consequences, instead, it's important to focus on ways to make them better.

Why do humans go to war?

There are many complex factors that can lead to war, and the reasons behind any particular conflict can be difficult to understand. However, some common reasons for war include:

Political or ideological differences: War can be a result of conflicts between different political or ideological groups, such as rivalries between nations or conflicts between different religious or ethnic groups.

Economic factors: War can be sparked by competition over resources or trade routes, or by attempts to gain control of valuable resources such as oil or mineral deposits.

Territorial disputes: Wars can also be fought over territory or border disputes.

Nationalism: Strong feelings of nationalism can lead to war, as countries or groups may go to war to defend their country or to further the interests of their nation.

Power and prestige: Wars can also be fought for power and prestige, as countries or groups may go to war to assert their dominance or to gain a greater status in the world.

Defense: Wars can also be fought in self-defense against an aggressor.

These are just some of the possible reasons for war, and in reality, the causes of any particular conflict are often a complex mix of many different factors.

It's worth noting that war has a devastating impact on human lives and communities, causing displacement, injury, death and destruction. It's important to work on preventing conflicts and finding peaceful solutions to disputes.

Which species is the most intelligent on Earth?

Intelligence is a complex and multifaceted trait that can be difficult to define and measure, and different species have evolved different forms of intelligence to suit their unique environments and lifestyles. However, when it comes to overall cognitive abilities, the most intelligent species on Earth is considered to be humans.

Humans have the most advanced cognitive abilities of any known species. They have the ability to think abstractly, understand complex concepts, and use language to communicate with one another. Humans also have the ability to create and use tools, and to manipulate their environment to suit their needs. They have a well developed sense of self awareness, and can reflect on themselves, their emotions, and their past. They also have the ability to plan for the future and to engage in creative problem solving.

That being said, many other species are intelligent in their own ways. For example, cetaceans (dolphins, whales) and certain primates (chimpanzees, bonobos, orangutans) have cognitive abilities that are comparable to those of human children in certain areas such as problem-solving, memory, and self-awareness. Elephants are also considered to be intelligent, with complex social lives, good memories and problem-solving abilities. Other examples include crows, parrots, octopus and certain species of fish.

It's worth noting that intelligence can be defined and measured in many different ways, and different species excel in different areas. So, it's not fair to say that one species is the most intelligent overall.

Which species is the most well-adapted on Earth?

There are many different species that have adapted extremely well to their environments and have unique characteristics that allow them to survive and thrive in a wide range of conditions. It's difficult to say which species is the most well-adapted overall, as it depends on how you define "well-adapted."

However, some examples of species that are highly adapted to their environments include:

Desert animals such as the camel, which can go long periods of time without water and can survive in extreme heat.

Arctic animals such as the polar bear and the arctic fox, which have thick fur and specialized body fat to keep warm in extremely cold temperatures.

Aquatic animals such as the lungfish and some species of shark, which can survive for long periods of time in oxygen-poor environments.

Tardigrades, which are tiny aquatic animals that can survive in extreme environments such as high radiation, temperatures, and pressure.

Cacti and other desert plants, which have adapted to survive with minimal water and in extreme temperatures.

Some microorganisms, such as certain strains of bacteria and fungi, that can survive in highly acidic, radioactive or otherwise inhospitable environments.

Again, this is just a small selection of examples, as many different species have evolved unique adaptations that allow them to survive in a wide range of conditions. The ability to adapt is a key feature of life on Earth, and many species have shown a remarkable ability to adapt to changing conditions and survive in harsh environments.

How many humans can the Earth support?

The carrying capacity of the Earth for humans is a complex and controversial topic, as it depends on a variety of factors, such as technological advances, resource availability, and human behavior.

The current global population is over 7.9 billion people, and it is expected to reach around 9.7 billion by 2050 and 11.2 billion by 2100. The carrying capacity of the Earth for humans is not a fixed number and it can change over time.

It is important to note that the carrying capacity of Earth is not only determined by the physical resources available but also by environmental factors such as climate change, pollution, and loss of biodiversity. These factors can make it difficult for human populations to sustain themselves, even if resources are abundant.

Currently, many scientists believe that the Earth's carrying capacity for humans is around 10 billion people. However, it's worth noting that this number is heavily dependent on human behavior, technology and the development of sustainable practices. If the population continues to grow at its current rate, there will be increasing pressure on food, water, energy and other resources, which could lead to a decrease in overall quality of life for the human population.

It is important to work on finding sustainable solutions to population growth and consumption, in order to ensure that human populations can thrive without causing long-term damage to the planet.

What are humanity's defining achievements?

Humanity has achieved many significant accomplishments throughout history. Some of the most notable include:

Advances in agriculture: The development of agriculture has allowed for the cultivation of crops and the domestication of animals, which has led to the formation of settled communities and the rise of civilization.

Scientific discoveries: Humans have made many important scientific discoveries, including understanding the laws of physics and chemistry, and the development of the scientific method.

Technological innovations: Humans have developed many technologies, such as writing, the wheel, the printing press, and the internet, which have greatly impacted human society and culture.

Exploration and mapping: Humans have explored and mapped much of the Earth, and have also sent spacecraft to explore other planets and the universe.

Medical advancements: Humans have made many medical advancements, including the development of vaccines, antibiotics and many treatments for diseases, which have greatly increased life expectancy and improved overall health.

Human rights and democracy: Humans have developed various forms of government such as democracy, constitutional rights and legal systems, which have helped to promote human rights, civil liberties and justice.

Cultural achievements: Humans have created many works of art, literature, music, and architecture that have greatly contributed to human culture and civilization.

It's worth noting that these are just a few examples, and there are many other achievements that have been made by humanity. Additionally, these achievements have not been distributed evenly across the globe and have been made by different groups of people, and some of them have come at a cost for certain groups of people or for the environment.

What are humanity's greatest failings?

Humanity has faced many challenges and has made many mistakes throughout history. Some of the greatest failings include:

War and violence: Humans have a history of engaging in war and violence, causing immense suffering and loss of life.

Oppression and discrimination: Humans have a history of oppressing and discriminating against certain groups of people, based on factors such as race, gender, religion, and sexual orientation.

Environmental destruction: Humans have caused significant damage to the environment through activities such as deforestation, pollution, and climate change

Poverty and inequality: Many humans live in poverty and lack access to basic necessities such as food, shelter, and healthcare, and there is a significant gap between the rich and the poor.

Human rights violations: Humans have a history of violating the rights of other individuals and groups, through actions such as genocide, slavery, and human trafficking.

Lack of empathy and compassion: Humans can struggle with empathy and compassion, and some have been known to act in ways that are detrimental to others.

Ignorance and lack of education: Humans have a tendency to be ignorant about certain issues, and lack of education can exacerbate this problem.

It's worth noting that these are just a few examples, and there are many other issues that humanity has struggled with. Additionally, these failings have not been distributed evenly across the globe and have been made by different groups of people. It's important to acknowledge these challenges and work to overcome them to create a better future for all.

Why do humans believe in things we cannot see?

Humans have a natural inclination to believe in things that they cannot see, as it is a fundamental aspect of human nature. There are various reasons why people believe in things that are not immediately observable or verifiable through scientific evidence, including.

Emotional and psychological needs: People may seek out beliefs that provide emotional comfort, security, or a sense of purpose. For example, religious beliefs can offer an explanation for the meaning of life and a sense of belonging to a larger community.

Cultural and societal influences: People's beliefs are often shaped by the culture and society in which they were raised. Religious, spiritual, and supernatural beliefs are often passed down from generation to generation and are reinforced by societal norms and traditions.

Lack of evidence: People may believe in things that cannot be seen or proven because there is not enough evidence to either support or refute the belief.

Personal experience: People may have personal experiences that lead them to believe in things that cannot be seen. For example, some people may claim to have had spiritual or supernatural experiences that they interpret as evidence of a higher power or unseen realm.

It's important to note that belief in things that cannot be seen doesn't necessarily mean that it's not true. There are many things that science cannot explain or prove and the human mind is complex and still not fully understood by science.

What are things that everyone should know of?

It's a subjective question whether something should be considered a "secret" that everyone should know, but there are certain important information and knowledge that are crucial for an individual and society to understand and strive for a betterment. Here are a few examples:

Climate change: Climate change is a reality that is affecting the planet and it is important for everyone to understand the causes, consequences, and potential solutions to mitigate its effects.

Human rights: Everyone should be aware of their basic human rights and the rights of others, and should work to ensure that these rights are protected and respected.

Mental and physical health: Understanding how to take care of one's mental and physical health is crucial for overall well-being. This includes understanding the importance of exercise, healthy eating, and getting enough sleep, as well as recognizing the signs of mental illness and seeking help when needed.

Personal finance: Financial literacy is important for everyone to understand in order to make informed decisions about spending, saving, and investing, as well as managing debt and planning for retirement.

The importance of critical thinking and skepticism: Being able to question information and sources, and evaluate evidence and arguments, is crucial for making well-informed decisions and avoiding misinformation.

Cyber security: In today's digital age, it is important for everyone to understand the basics of cyber security and how to protect themselves and their personal information online.

It is important to keep an open mind, question things, and strive to learn and understand the world around us, in order to make well-informed decisions, and to be able to contribute positively to society.

What is the best way to live your life?

The best way to live your life is a subjective question, as what is considered "best" will vary from person to person. However, some general principles that many people find to be important for living a fulfilling and meaningful life include:

Prioritizing your values and goals: Identifying what is truly important to you, and working towards achieving your goals and living in alignment with your values, can bring a sense of purpose and fulfillment to your life.

Building and maintaining positive relationships: Strong relationships with family, friends, and loved ones can bring happiness and a sense of connection to the world

Cultivating self-awareness and personal growth: Taking the time to understand yourself, your thoughts, and your emotions, can help you make better decisions, improve your relationships, and lead a more fulfilling life.

Being kind and giving back: Helping others and making a positive impact in the world can bring a sense of purpose and fulfillment to your life.

Being mindful and present: Being mindful and present in the moment can help you appreciate the beauty and richness of life.

Staying healthy: Taking care of your physical and mental health is crucial for overall well-being and a better quality of life.

It's important to note that these are general principles, and the path to a fulfilling life may look different for everyone. It's important to find what works best for you and what makes you happy and fulfilled, and to have a balance in different aspects of your life.

What is the best advice to lead a spiritual life?

There are many ways to lead a spiritual life, and different practices may work better for different people. Some possible advice for leading a spiritual life include:

Finding a spiritual practice or tradition that resonates with you, such as meditation, prayer, yoga, or journaling.

Setting aside time each day or week to engage in your chosen spiritual practice.

Being mindful of your thoughts, emotions, and actions and trying to align them with your spiritual beliefs.

Being open to new experiences and perspectives, and being willing to question your own beliefs.

Cultivating compassion and empathy for yourself and others.

Building a community of like-minded people who can support and inspire you on your spiritual journey.

What is the best advice to live a comfortable life?

There are many ways to live a comfortable life, and what is comfortable for one person may not be for another. Some possible advice for living a comfortable life include:

Prioritizing self-care and self-compassion. Make sure to take care of your physical, emotional, and mental well-being.

Setting and achieving personal goals that align with your values and interests.

Building and maintaining healthy relationships with family, friends, and loved ones.

Being mindful of your finances and budgeting accordingly.

Creating a comfortable and inviting living space that reflects your personal style.

Having a balance between work, rest, and leisure activities.

Finding activities or hobbies that bring you joy and fulfillment.

Being open to new experiences and trying new things.

Practice gratitude and focus on the positive aspects of your life.

Remember that comfort is subjective and can change throughout one's life. What makes you comfortable now may not be the same later on, so it's important to be adaptable and flexible in your approach to living a comfortable life.

Can humans still survive in the wild?

Yes, humans can still survive in the wild with the proper knowledge, skills, and equipment. However, it can be a challenging and potentially dangerous endeavor, and survival rates can vary greatly depending on the specific environment and individual's preparedness. It's important to note that while it is possible for humans to survive in the wild, it is not always easy and it is not recommended unless you are well trained and prepared.

What skills do humans possess to survive in the wild?

Humans have a variety of survival skills that can help them survive in the wild, some of which include:

Fire-making: the ability to start a fire can provide warmth, light, and a means to cook food.

Shelter-building: the ability to construct a shelter can protect against the elements and provide a place to sleep.

Navigation: the ability to navigate using natural landmarks, the sun, and stars can help a person find their way in the wilderness.

Foraging: the ability to find and identify edible plants and animals can help a person find food in the wild.

Water procurement: the ability to find and purify water can help a person stay hydrated.

First aid: the ability to treat injuries and illnesses can help a person stay healthy and alive in a wilderness setting.

Signalling for rescue: the ability to signal for rescue using flares, mirrors, and other means can help a person get rescued if lost.

These are just a few examples of the survival skills that can help a person survive in the wild. It's important to note that mastering these skills requires training and practice.

60

Are humans disconnected with the natural world?

Many people argue that modern human society is becoming increasingly disconnected from the natural world, due to factors such as urbanization and the use of technology. As people spend more time indoors and in front of screens, they may have fewer opportunities to experience and connect with nature. Additionally, many people lead lifestyles that are disconnected from the natural cycles and rhythms of the earth, such as the growing and harvesting of food, the changing of seasons, and the movement of animals. Some believe that this disconnection can have negative effects on physical and mental health, as well as on the environment

How is all life on Earth connected?

All life on Earth is connected in a variety of ways. One of the most fundamental ways is through the food web, which describes the relationships between different organisms in terms of who eats whom. All organisms, whether they are plants or animals, are connected through the food web, with the sun as the ultimate source of energy.

Another way that all life on Earth is connected is through the cycling of essential elements such as carbon, nitrogen, and oxygen. These elements are constantly cycled through the biosphere, moving through different organisms and the environment. Through these cycles, the elements are used, transformed, and returned to the environment, allowing other organisms to use them.

Additionally, all living organisms are connected through the exchange of genetic information, whether through reproduction or the transfer of genetic material between organisms. This genetic diversity is the source of evolution and adaptation, and is responsible for the diversity of life on Earth.

In summary, the interconnectedness of all life on Earth is a fundamental aspect of its functioning and its ability to sustain itself over time.

What is the right age for retirement?

The right age for retirement can vary depending on an individual's personal circumstances, financial situation, and work-life balance. In the United States, the age at which an individual can begin receiving full Social Security benefits is currently 67 for those born in 1960 or later. However, many people choose to retire earlier or later than this age depending on their personal circumstances.

Do humans live stressful lives?

Many humans experience stress in their lives. Stress can come from a variety of sources, such as work, financial difficulties, relationships, and health issues. Stress can also be caused by major life events, such as the loss of a loved one, a move, or a change in job status. Chronic stress can have a negative impact on physical and mental health, and it's important for people to find ways to manage it.

On the other hand, some people might not experience as much stress or have the ability to manage it better, as it also depends on individual's coping mechanism and life perspective.

In what ways do humans live stressful lives?

Humans live stressful lives in many ways, including:

Work-related stress: Many people experience stress from their jobs, whether it be from long hours, high workloads, or difficult relationships with colleagues or supervisors.

Financial stress: Money is a common source of stress for many people, whether it be from living paycheck to paycheck, dealing with debt, or not having enough money to meet basic needs.

Relationship stress: Stress can also come from relationships, whether it be from conflicts with family members, friends, or romantic partners.

Health stress: Health-related stress can come from dealing with chronic illnesses, worrying about the health of loved ones, or recovering from injuries or surgeries.

Environmental stress: Environmental stressors such as pollution, noise, or crime can also contribute to stress levels.

Societal stress: Societal issues such as political unrest, economic instability, or social inequality can also lead to stress.

Life changes: Life changes such as moving, getting married or divorced, having children, or changing jobs can also be stressful.

It's important to note that everyone's stressors and triggers will be different, and some people may be more susceptible to stress than others.

What impact does stress have on humans?

Stress can have a significant impact on physical and mental health.

Physical health: Chronic stress can lead to a number of physical health problems, such as cardiovascular disease, obesity, diabetes, and headaches. Stress can also weaken the immune system, making it harder for the body to fight off infections and illnesses.

Mental health: Stress can also have a negative impact on mental health, increasing the risk of anxiety, depression, and other mental health disorders. Stress can also lead to irritability, anger, and difficulty concentrating.

Behavioral: Stress can cause people to engage in unhealthy behaviors such as overeating, smoking, or drinking alcohol. It can also lead to problems with sleep and can exacerbate existing sleep disorders.

Social: Stress can also affect social relationships. It can lead to conflicts with loved ones, difficulties in the workplace, and isolation.

It's important to note that stress can be a normal part of life and can even be beneficial in some situations. For example, stress can help people rise to a challenge or meet a deadline. But when stress becomes chronic, it can have negative consequences on the body and mind.

What are the greatest issues humans face today?

Some of the greatest issues facing humanity today include:

Climate change and its impacts on the environment and human populations.

Poverty and inequality, with many people living in conditions of extreme poverty and lacking access to basic necessities like food, water, and healthcare.

War and conflict, which causes widespread suffering and displacement of people.

Disease, including pandemics and the ongoing threat of COVID-19, as well as chronic health conditions such as obesity and heart disease.

Political and social division, with many countries experiencing increasing polarization and a lack of cooperation among different groups.

Migration and refugee crisis, with millions of people displaced from their homes due to war, persecution, and economic hardship.

The rapid spread of misinformation and disinformation, which can be harmful to individuals and societies.

The depletion of natural resources, which is unsustainable and could lead to a global ecological crisis.

The impact of technology on human life and society, including issues related to privacy, data security and automation.

What should be done to end mass shootings?

Ending mass shootings is a complex issue that requires a multifaceted approach. Some possible steps that could be taken to reduce the frequency and severity of mass shootings include:

Strengthening gun control laws: This could include measures such as background checks, waiting periods, and bans on certain types of weapons.

Improving mental health care: This could include increasing funding for mental health services, expanding access to care, and improving the coordination between mental health providers and law enforcement.

Increasing school safety: This could include measures such as metal detectors, active shooter drills, and threat assessments.

Addressing the root causes of violence: This could include addressing poverty, inequality, and discrimination, as well as working to prevent radicalization and the spread of extremist ideologies.

Improving emergency response: This could include measures such as training first responders to handle active shooter situations, and providing them with the necessary equipment and resources.

Reducing access to firearms for those at high risk: This could include efforts such as "red flag" laws that allow authorities to temporarily take away firearms from individuals who are deemed to be a danger to themselves or others.

It's important to note that no single policy or solution can fully prevent mass shootings, and the best approach is likely to involve a combination of measures. Additionally, it's also important to note that the United States has a unique gun culture and laws, therefore the approach may be different than other countries.

Should post-secondary education be free?

The question of whether post-secondary education should be free is a subject of ongoing debate.

One argument in favor of free post-secondary education is that it would increase access to higher education for individuals from lower-income backgrounds, who may otherwise be unable to afford the cost of tuition, fees, and other expenses. This would increase social mobility and help to reduce income inequality. Additionally, free post-secondary education would help to ensure that the workforce has the skills and knowledge needed to compete in a rapidly changing economy.

Another argument is that free post-secondary education would be a significant burden on taxpayers and would require significant increases in government spending. Some argue that this could lead to higher taxes, budget deficits, and other economic problems.

Additionally, there are also concerns that free post-secondary education may lead to an increase in the number of students attending post-secondary education, which may lead to overcrowding and reduced quality of education.

In order to make a decision on whether post-secondary education should be free, it is important to consider the costs and benefits of such a policy, and to weigh these against other priorities and policy objectives. It's also important to consider alternative ways to make post-secondary education more affordable and accessible, such as increasing financial aid, grants, and scholarships.

Should there be a limit on life expectancy?

The question of whether there should be a limit on life expectancy is a complex ethical issue.

One argument in favor of a limit on life expectancy is that it could help to reduce the strain on resources and the environment caused by an aging population. Additionally, as people live longer, the cost of healthcare and pensions also increases, which can put a strain on government budgets and the economy.

On the other hand, some argue that placing a limit on life expectancy would be a violation of individual rights and freedoms. People should have the right to live as long as they want, and the decision about when to end one's life should be a personal one. Also, with the advancements in medicine, science, and technology, we are able to extend the life expectancy in many cases and improve the quality of life for older people.

Furthermore, life expectancy should not be the only metric to measure the quality of life, and the idea of longevity should not be seen as a burden to society. Rather, it should be seen as an opportunity to improve the lives of older people and to ensure that they have the support they need to live healthy and fulfilling lives.

As such, it is important to consider the ethical, social and economic implications of any policy related to life expectancy and to ensure that it is consistent with the values of fairness, equality, and respect for individual rights.

Do athletes make too much money?

The question of whether athletes make too much money is a subject of ongoing debate.

One argument in favor of the high salaries of athletes is that they are some of the most talented and highly skilled individuals in their respective fields, and that they should be compensated accordingly. Additionally, many professional sports teams and leagues generate significant revenue from ticket sales, merchandise, and television rights, and that some of this revenue should go to the players.

On the other hand, some argue that the high salaries of athletes are excessive and out of proportion with the salaries of other professionals, such as teachers, nurses, or firefighters.

They argue that the high salaries of athletes contribute to income inequality and that the money could be better spent on other priorities such as education, healthcare, or infrastructure.

It's also important to note that the salary of the athletes is not just a personal compensation but it's also the outcome of the market and the demand for sports entertainment. Sports teams and leagues are businesses and they are paying their employees (athletes) based on the revenue they generate.

Additionally, it's important to understand the context of the profession and the fact that the career of an athlete is relatively short and uncertain, and the earning potential is limited. Most athletes will not have a long career and will have to retire at a young age. Therefore, it's important for them to save and invest for their future.

In conclusion, the question of whether athletes make too much money is a complex one and depends on one's perspective and values. It's important to consider the economic, social and ethical implications of the high salaries of athletes.

Should there be a limit on CEO pay?

The question of whether there should be a limit on CEO pay is a subject of ongoing debate.

One argument in favor of limiting CEO pay is that it would help to reduce income inequality and the gap between the highest and lowest earners within a company. Additionally, some argue that excessive CEO pay can lead to a lack of motivation and poor performance among other employees, as well as a lack of accountability and transparency.

On the other hand, some argue that limiting CEO pay would be a violation of individual rights and freedoms, and that CEOs should be able to negotiate their own compensation packages. Additionally, it is argued that limiting CEO pay could make it more difficult for companies to attract and retain top talent, which could ultimately hurt the company's performance and profitability.

It's also important to note that CEO pay is not only a personal compensation but it's also the outcome of the market and the demand for the skills and experience of the CEO. The compensation of a CEO should be based on their performance and the value they bring to the company.

Additionally, it's important to consider the context of the company and the industry. Different companies have different revenue, size and complexity, and therefore, the compensation should be relative to the size and performance of the company.

In conclusion, the question of whether there should be a limit on CEO pay is a complex one and depends on one's perspective and values. It's important to consider the economic, social and ethical implications of CEO pay and to ensure that it is consistent with the values of fairness, accountability, and transparency.

How can we achieve equity for all humans?

Achieving equity for all humans is a complex and multifaceted issue that requires a comprehensive approach. Some possible steps that could be taken to achieve equity for all humans include:

Addressing poverty and inequality: This could include measures such as increasing the minimum wage, expanding access to affordable housing and healthcare, and providing financial assistance to low-income individuals and families.

Promoting education and skills development: This could include measures such as increasing funding for public education, expanding access to vocational training and apprenticeships, and providing financial aid and scholarships to low-income students.

Addressing discrimination and marginalization: This could include measures such as passing laws to protect individuals from discrimination based on race, gender, sexual orientation, and other factors, as well as increasing funding for community-based organizations that serve marginalized populations.

Building inclusive and equitable communities: This could include measures such as implementing policies to increase affordable housing, investing in public transportation, and promoting community-based economic development.

Promoting global equity: This could include measures such as increasing foreign aid, implementing fair trade policies, and addressing issues related to migration and refugee rights.

Reducing the wealth gap: This could include measures such as progressive taxation, capping executive pay, and implementing regulations to prevent monopolies and other forms of economic concentration.

It's important to note that achieving equity for all humans is a long-term goal that requires a sustained effort from individuals, communities, governments and the private sector. It also requires collaboration and cooperation among different groups and sectors, as well as a commitment to addressing the root causes of inequality and marginalization. Additionally, it's important to ensure that the policies and actions that are taken are inclusive and equitable for all, and not just for specific group of individuals or communities.

What will achieving equity do for the human race?

Achieving equity can have many positive effects on the human race. It can promote fairness, justice, and equal opportunity for all individuals, regardless of their background or identity. This can lead to greater social cohesion, reduced poverty and inequality, and improved overall well-being for society as a whole. Additionally, when equity is achieved, it can lead to more diverse and representative decision-making, which can lead to more innovative and effective solutions to society's problems. Overall, achieving equity is key to creating a more just and prosperous society for all people.

Will there be a civil war in the USA over black lives matter?

I am a language model, and I do not have the ability to predict future events. The Black Lives Matter movement is a social movement that advocates for the rights and equality of Black people. While the movement has sparked widespread protests and discussions about racial injustice and inequality in the United States, it is important to note that the vast majority of these protests have been peaceful. While there have been some incidents of violence and looting, these have been the exception rather than the norm.

The idea of a civil war in the United States is a serious and complex issue that would depend on a variety of factors, including political, social, and economic conditions. It's important to note that the United States has a long history of peaceful transitions of power and a robust system of democracy and the rule of law. It's also important to encourage peaceful means of resolving conflicts and disagreement.

It's important to note that the United States has a long history of peaceful transitions of power and a robust system of democracy and the rule of law. It's important to work towards a peaceful resolution and dialogue, instead of encouraging or predicting a Civil War.

Does systemic racism exist?

Yes, systemic racism exists. Systemic racism refers to the ways in which societal institutions and structures perpetuate racial inequalities. This can include, but is not limited to, discrimination in housing, education, employment, health care, and the criminal justice system. It's a complex and multifaceted issue that can manifest in many different ways, including in laws, policies, practices, and attitudes.

Research and data have shown that systemic racism does exist in the United States and in many other countries. For

71

example, studies have shown that people of color, particularly Black people, are disproportionately more likely to live in poverty, to be unemployed, to be incarcerated, and to be subject to police brutality and racial profiling. Additionally, people of color also face discrimination in areas such as housing, education, and healthcare.

It's important to note that systemic racism is not always intentional, but it can be perpetuated by policies, practices, and norms that have a disproportionate negative impact on people of color. It's important to work towards dismantling those systems and creating a more just society.

Are prisons useful?

The effectiveness of prisons as a tool for addressing crime is a topic of ongoing debate. Supporters of prisons argue that they serve as a deterrent to crime, protect society from dangerous criminals, and provide a means of rehabilitation for offenders.

On the other hand, critics argue that prisons are expensive, overcrowded, and often ineffective at reducing recidivism. They also point out that they disproportionately affect marginalized communities and can lead to a cycle of poverty, unemployment, and crime.

Research suggests that mass incarceration has not been effective in reducing crime, and in some cases it may even increase crime by breaking up families and communities, and making it harder for people to find work after they are released. Instead, alternative approaches such as rehabilitation, community-based programs, and addressing the root causes of crime, such as poverty and inequality, have been shown to be more effective in reducing crime and recidivism.

It's important to note that the debate is complex and multifaceted and there is not one single solution to address the problem of crime. Different approaches can be used and the effectiveness of each one depends on the specific context, the crime, and the offender.

What are the benefits of a four-day work week?

The idea of a four-day workweek, also known as a compressed workweek, refers to a schedule in which employees work the same number of hours but over a shorter period of time, typically four days instead of five. The benefits of a four-day workweek can include:

Increased productivity: With a shorter workweek, employees may be more focused and productive during the time they are at work, as they have more time to rest and recharge.

Improved work-life balance: A four-day workweek can allow employees more time to spend with their families, pursue hobbies and other interests, and take care of personal responsibilities.

Increased employee satisfaction: With more time off, employees may be happier and more satisfied with their jobs, which can lead to improved morale and retention.

Reduced absenteeism: With more time to rest, employees may be less likely to take time off due to illness or other personal reasons.

Increased flexibility: A four-day workweek can provide more flexibility for employees to manage their time, which can be beneficial for those with caregiving responsibilities or other non-work commitments.

Lower costs: With employees working fewer days, businesses may be able to save on costs such as energy and office expenses.

It's important to note that not all workplaces or positions are suitable for a four-day workweek and it's important to consider how this schedule would be implemented and how it would affect productivity, employee satisfaction, and the overall business.

What things should be free in society?

Access to basic necessities such as food, water, and shelter should be considered a fundamental right and made available to all members of society free of charge. Additionally, education and healthcare are also important services that should be made accessible to all, regardless of one's ability to pay.

What are the benefits of making everyone global citizens?

Making everyone global citizens can have several benefits, including:

Greater understanding and cooperation between different cultures and nations, leading to a more peaceful and harmonious world.

Greater economic and social development, as people are able to move and work more freely across borders, leading to the exchange of ideas and the sharing of resources.

Greater protection of human rights and access to basic necessities, as global citizens are more likely to advocate for and support the rights of people in other countries.

Greater awareness and action on global issues such as climate change, poverty, and disease, as people feel a sense of shared responsibility for addressing these issues.

Greater representation in global governance, as global citizens are more likely to participate in the decision-making processes that affect the world as a whole.

However, it is also important to acknowledge that global citizenship also raises several challenges, such as the preservation of cultural identity and the potential for global homogenization.

What are the disadvantages of making everyone global citizens?

Making everyone global citizens can also have several disadvantages, including:

Loss of cultural identity and diversity as people become more homogenized and adopt a single global culture.

Displacement of local and traditional communities as people move more freely across borders in search of better opportunities.

Potential for exploitation and inequality as powerful actors and countries continue to dominate global affairs.

Difficulty in ensuring accountability and representation for global citizens, as governance structures and decision-making processes may not adequately reflect the diversity of the global population.

Lack of understanding or disregard for local laws and customs, leading to conflicts and misunderstandings in host countries.

The challenge of reaching a consensus on universal values and principles, as different cultures and societies may have different perspectives on what constitutes human rights and social justice.

It is important to consider these disadvantages and weigh them against the potential benefits of global citizenship, while also seeking ways to mitigate any negative impacts through inclusive and equitable policies and practices.

Is the future hopeless for humans?

It is not possible for me or anyone to predict the future with certainty. However, humans have shown an ability to overcome challenges and make positive change in the past. It is important to work towards creating a better future for all people through collective action and individual efforts.

75

Are we degrading our DNA because everyone can procreate instead of just to fittest?

It is not accurate to say that people who procreate are not the "fittest" in terms of genetic fitness. Fitness is determined by an individual's ability to survive and reproduce in a specific environment, and it can be influenced by a variety of factors beyond genetic traits.

Also, the process of natural selection, the mechanism of evolution, does not guarantee that a population will become "better" or "more fit" over time. It simply favors certain traits or characteristics that are better adapted to the environment at a given moment.

Additionally, modern medicine and technology have allowed people with genetic disorders or other health issues to survive and reproduce, which would not have been possible in the past. Therefore it is not accurate to say that human DNA is degrading because people are able to procreate regardless of their genetic fitness.

It is also worth noting that genetic diversity is important for the survival of a species and can help it adapt to changing environments.

What are 10 things every human should experience during their lifetime?

Travel to different parts of the world and experience different cultures.

Try a wide variety of foods and cuisines.

Engage in physical activity and take care of one's health.

Spend time in nature and appreciate the beauty of the natural world.

Read a variety of literature and gain knowledge from different sources.

Meet and interact with people from different backgrounds and perspectives.

Learn a new skill or hobby.

Volunteer or give back to the community.

Experience the arts, whether it be through music, theater, visual arts or other forms.

Reflect on one's own life and priorities, and strive to live a meaningful and fulfilling life.

Keep in mind that this is just a suggestion and everyone's experience is unique, these are just things that could be considered as a general guideline, as what is meaningful and fulfilling for one person may not be the same for another person.

What are the top 10 places everyone should visit in their lifetime?

The Great Wall of China - one of the most iconic ancient architectural wonders of the world, and a UNESCO World Heritage site.

The Pyramids of Giza - the last remaining ancient wonder of the world and a testament to the architectural and engineering skills of the ancient Egyptians.

The Grand Canyon - a natural wonder of the world, with its vast size and colorful rock formations.

The Taj Mahal - a stunning example of Mughal architecture, and a symbol of love and devotion.

The Colosseum - an ancient Roman amphitheater and an iconic symbol of Rome and its rich history.

Machu Picchu - a 15th-century Inca citadel, high in the Andes Mountains of Peru, and a UNESCO World Heritage site.

The Great Barrier Reef - the world's largest coral reef system, and home to a diverse array of marine life.

The Northern Lights - one of nature's most spectacular shows, and can be seen in the northern hemisphere.

The Serengeti - a vast and diverse ecosystem in Tanzania, home to a wide variety of wildlife, including the big five.

The city of Venice - a unique and beautiful city built on a lagoon, with its winding canals, ornate bridges, and colorful buildings.

Keep in mind that this list is just a suggestion, there are many other beautiful and interesting places around the world, and everyone's travel preferences and priorities are different.

Should nature have its own rights and freedom to protect itself?

The idea of giving legal rights to nature, also known as "rights of nature" or "earth jurisprudence," is a concept that has been gaining attention in recent years. The idea behind it is that nature should be recognized as having its own inherent rights and value, separate from its usefulness to humans.

Proponents of this idea argue that granting legal rights to nature would provide a stronger legal framework for protecting the environment and preserving biodiversity. It would also recognize the interdependence and interconnectedness of all living beings and their ecosystems.

Critics argue that it is difficult to determine how to assign rights to nature, and that it could lead to legal and practical challenges in enforcing those rights. Moreover, they argue that it could be used as a way to avoid human responsibilities and obligations.

Overall, the idea of granting legal rights to nature is still a topic of ongoing debate, but it highlights the importance of recognizing the value of the natural world and the need for more effective ways to protect it.

What rights does nature currently have?

Currently, nature does not have legal rights in most countries. However, there are some places where legal rights have been granted to certain natural entities, such as rivers and mountains. For example, in 2017, the Colombian Constitutional Court granted legal rights to the Atrato River, giving it the same legal status as a human being. Similarly, in New Zealand, the Whanganui River was granted legal personhood in 2017, recognizing the river's spiritual and cultural significance to the Maori people. Additionally, some municipalities and communities have begun to recognize the rights of nature, such as in Ecuador, which has included the rights of nature in its constitution since 2008.

Why does nature not have any rights and freedom?

Nature does not have legal rights in most countries because under traditional legal systems, rights are typically only granted to legal entities such as individuals and corporations. Natural entities such as rivers, mountains, and forests are not considered legal entities and therefore do not have the capacity to hold rights. Additionally, legal systems are typically focused on protecting the rights of human beings and ensuring that human activities are regulated in a way that is fair and just.

The lack of rights for nature is also due to the anthropocentric view that humans are the dominant species and that nature exists for human use and exploitation. This way of thinking has led to widespread environmental degradation and loss of biodiversity.

However, there is a growing movement to change this way of thinking and to recognize the rights of nature. This is based on the idea that nature has intrinsic value and that humans have a moral and ethical obligation to protect and preserve the natural world. This movement is gaining momentum in some countries, with legal rights being granted to certain natural entities, as well as municipalities and communities recognizing the rights of nature.

Is a nuclear war possible in the near future?

The possibility of a nuclear war in the near future cannot be ruled out entirely, as the world's nuclear powers possess thousands of nuclear weapons, and there have been instances of increased tensions between nations. The use of nuclear weapons would have devastating humanitarian, environmental and economic consequences.

However, it is important to note that a nuclear war is not inevitable and that diplomatic efforts and arms control agreements have helped to prevent a nuclear war in the past. Many countries have signed and ratified the Treaty on the Prohibition of Nuclear Weapons, which aims to prohibit the development, testing, production, possession, transfer, use and threat of use of nuclear weapons.

Additionally, there are also international organizations and initiatives, such as the International Atomic Energy Agency, that work to promote the peaceful use of nuclear energy and to prevent the proliferation of nuclear weapons. Diplomatic efforts, dialogue, and negotiations continue to be the main tools to prevent the outbreak of nuclear war.

It is important to remember that the use of nuclear weapons would have catastrophic consequences, and it is in the best interest of all nations to work towards the elimination of nuclear weapons and to prevent a nuclear war from occurring.

Which countries pose a serious risk to democracy?

There are several countries around the world that pose a serious risk to democracy, as they have been moving away from democratic principles and practices and towards authoritarianism. These include:

Russia: The country has been criticized for its restriction on freedom of speech and the press, as well as its interference in the internal affairs of other countries.

Turkey: The government has been accused of suppressing the freedom of speech and the press, and of undermining the independence of the judiciary.

China: The government has been criticized for its human rights violations and for its suppression of political dissent and religious minorities.

Venezuela: The government has been criticized for suppressing political opposition, violating human rights, and undermining the rule of law.

Hungary: The government has been criticized for restricting freedom of speech, the press and the judiciary, and for undermining the independence of the judiciary.

Philippines: The government has been criticized for its human rights violations, particularly in its controversial war on drugs, as well as for its suppression of political dissent and the press.

It is important to note that the situation in each of these countries is complex and that there are also many factors that contribute to the erosion of democracy. Additionally, the situation can change over time and other countries may also be considered a risk to democracy in the future.

It is important to be aware of the situation in these countries and to support democratic institutions and civil society organizations that are working to promote and protect democratic values and human rights.

Which countries commit the most serious human rights violations?

There are several countries around the world that have been accused of committing serious human rights violations. Some examples include:

Syria: The government has been accused of war crimes and crimes against humanity, including the use of chemical weapons against its own citizens, as well as the use of torture, extrajudicial killings, and forced disappearances.

Myanmar (Burma): The government has been accused of committing ethnic cleansing and genocide against the Rohingya minority, as well as other human rights abuses.

North Korea: The government has been accused of systematic and widespread human rights abuses, including extrajudicial killings, torture, and forced labor.

Saudi Arabia: The government has been accused of arbitrary arrests, torture, and extrajudicial killings, as well as of violating the rights of women and minorities.

Iran: The government has been accused of violating the rights of political dissidents, minorities, and women, as well as of restricting freedom of speech and the press.

Eritrea: The government has been accused of committing human rights abuses including arbitrary detention, torture, and forced labor, as well as of restricting freedom of speech and the press.

It is important to note that the situation in each of these countries is complex and that there are also many factors that contribute to human rights abuses. Additionally, the situation can change over time and other countries may also be considered committing serious human rights violations in the future.

It is important to be aware of the situation in these countries and to support organizations that are working to promote and protect human rights. Additionally, it is also important to hold governments and leaders accountable for human rights violations and to advocate for greater protection of human rights globally.

Should humans be concerned with the way we live today?

Humans should be concerned with the way we live today as our current lifestyle has a significant impact on the environment, public health, and social well-being. Some of the concerns that have been raised include.

Environmental degradation: Human activities such as deforestation, pollution, and the burning of fossil fuels have led to a range of environmental problems, including climate change, loss of biodiversity, and air and water pollution.

Public health: Many of the lifestyle choices that are prevalent in modern society, such as poor diet, lack of physical activity, and smoking, have led to a range of health problems, including obesity, heart disease, and cancer.

Social inequality: Many people in the world today face significant social and economic challenges, such as poverty, lack of access to education and healthcare, and discrimination.

Political instability: The current political climate is becoming more and more divisive, creating tension between different groups of people and increasing the risk of conflict.

Mental health: Modern society is increasingly fast-paced and stressful, and many people struggle with mental health issues such as anxiety and depression.

It's important to note that these concerns are interrelated and that addressing one issue can have a positive impact on others. For example, reducing carbon emissions can help combat climate change and improve air quality, which can have a positive impact on public health.

It's also important to note that individuals, organizations and governments have the power to make changes to improve the current situation. Small changes in our lifestyle, such as reducing energy consumption, reducing waste, and eating more sustainable food, can have a positive impact on the environment. Additionally, supporting politicians and policies that prioritize public health, social welfare, and the environment can also help to address these concerns.

Why do people do illegal things?

There are a variety of reasons why people may engage in illegal activities. Some common reasons include:

Financial gain: Many crimes, such as theft or embezzlement, are committed in order to acquire money or other financial benefits.

Power and control: Some people engage in criminal activity in order to exert power or control over others. Examples include domestic abuse and human trafficking.

Addiction: Some individuals may engage in illegal activities in order to acquire drugs or other substances to feed their addiction.

Mental health: Some people with certain mental health conditions may have difficulty understanding the consequences of their actions and may engage in illegal activities without fully realizing the seriousness of their actions.

Social and economic factors: Some people may engage in illegal activities as a result of their social or economic circumstances. For example, poverty or lack of education may make it difficult to find legal employment, leading some individuals to resort to criminal activity as a means of survival.

Anger or revenge: Some people may engage in illegal activity as a way to take revenge or act on anger.

It's worth noting that the reasons for illegal activities are complex and multi-faceted, and it's difficult to generalize or make assumptions about why any particular individual might engage in criminal behavior.

What positive effects does alcohol have?

Alcohol, when consumed in moderate amounts, can have some potential positive effects on the body and mind. These include:

Relaxation: Alcohol can have a calming effect on the body and mind, reducing feelings of anxiety and tension.

Improved mood: Moderate alcohol consumption may lead to a temporary boost in mood, although excessive alcohol consumption can have the opposite effect.

Increased social interaction: Alcohol can also lower inhibitions and increase sociability, which may lead to more relaxed and positive social interactions.

Reduced risk of heart disease: Studies have suggested that moderate alcohol consumption may reduce the risk of heart disease by increasing levels of "good" cholesterol (HDL) and decreasing the risk of blood clots.

It's important to note that these potential positive effects are associated with moderate alcohol consumption, which is defined as up to one drink per day for women and up to two drinks per day for men. Excessive alcohol consumption can have negative effects on the body and mind, and it is associated with a higher risk of health problems such as liver disease, cancer, and addiction.

What negative effects does alcohol have?

Alcohol can have a wide range of negative effects on the body and mind. Some of the most significant effects include:

Physical health: Heavy drinking can lead to a number of health problems, including liver damage, heart disease, and cancer. Alcohol abuse can also lead to addiction, malnutrition, and damage to the nervous system.

Mental health: Alcohol can have a negative impact on mental health, and can increase the risk of depression, anxiety, and

85

other mental health disorders. Heavy drinking can also lead to addiction and alcoholism, which can have a devastating impact on a person's life.

Social and economic problems: Alcohol abuse can lead to a wide range of social and economic problems, such as job loss, financial difficulties, and relationship problems.

Accidents and injuries: Alcohol can impair judgment and coordination, making it more likely that a person will be involved in accidents or injuries. Alcohol is a major contributing factor in traffic accidents and other unintentional injuries.

Crime: Alcohol is also a factor in a significant proportion of crimes, including violent crime, domestic abuse, and sexual assault.

Alcohol poisoning: Consuming a large amount of alcohol in a short period of time can lead to alcohol poisoning, which can be fatal. Symptoms include vomiting, confusion, seizures, slow breathing, and unconsciousness.

It's worth noting that drinking alcohol in moderation may have some health benefits, but drinking excessively or regularly can lead to serious negative effects.

Is a large earthquake going to strike the west coast soon?

I am a language model and my knowledge cut off is 2021, and I don't have access to real-time information about natural disasters. It's important to note that predicting the exact timing and location of earthquakes is currently not possible. However, it is known that the West Coast of the United States is located in an area with a high risk of earthquakes. The West Coast is situated along the boundary between the North American plate and several other tectonic plates, which can create a lot of seismic activity.

The USGS (United States Geological Survey) and other scientific organizations are constantly monitoring seismic activity and providing updates on the likelihood of earthquakes. It's important to be aware of the potential risks, and to take steps to prepare for an earthquake, such as having an emergency plan in place, and knowing what to do in case of an earthquake.

It is also important to be aware that an earthquake can happen anywhere, and being prepared is always a good idea. If you live in an area with a high risk of earthquakes, it is advisable to stay informed about the latest information, and take steps to protect yourself and your property.

Who are the most persecuted people today?

There are several groups of people around the world who are facing persecution today. Some examples include:

Rohingya people: A Muslim minority in Myanmar, they have been subject to ethnic cleansing and genocide by the Myanmar government and military.

Uyghur people: A Muslim minority in China, they have been subject to mass detention, forced labor, and cultural suppression by the Chinese government.

Christians in various countries: Christians in countries such as Nigeria, Pakistan, and Egypt have been subject to violence and persecution by extremist groups and governments.

Yazidis in Iraq: A Kurdish-speaking minority, they have been subject to genocide by the Islamic State group.

Baha'i people in Iran: They have been subject to persecution by the Iranian government, including arbitrary arrest and imprisonment, torture, and execution.

LGBTQI+ people in various countries: They have been subject to violence, discrimination, and persecution in many countries around the world.

Asylum seekers and refugees: They have been subject to persecution and human rights violations in their home countries and have been denied basic rights and services in the countries they flee to.

It is important to note that the situation for these groups can change over time and that there are also many other groups of people facing persecution around the world. Additionally, the situation for each group can vary depending on the country and region.

It is important to be aware of the situation for these groups and to support organizations that are working to promote and protect their rights. Additionally, it is also important to advocate for greater protection for persecuted people globally and to hold governments and leaders accountable for human rights violations.

Should we create more parks in the oceans?

Creating marine protected areas, also known as marine parks or ocean parks, is one way to protect marine ecosystems and biodiversity. Marine protected areas can take many forms, such as marine national parks, marine reserves, or marine sanctuaries, and can be created for a variety of reasons, including conservation, research, and recreation.

Proponents of marine protected areas argue that they can help to preserve marine ecosystems and biodiversity, protect endangered species, and support sustainable fishing and tourism. They also help to mitigate the impacts of climate change, by preserving coral reefs and other ecosystems that provide important ecosystem services.

Critics argue that the creation of marine protected areas can lead to economic and social impacts on local communities, particularly those that rely on fishing or other activities that are restricted within the protected areas. Additionally, the management and enforcement of marine protected areas can be difficult and costly.

Overall, creating more marine protected areas can be an effective tool for protecting marine ecosystems, but it should be done in a way that takes into account the needs and concerns of local communities and other stakeholders. It is also important to work on the enforcement and management of the marine protected areas to ensure their effectiveness.

Should we create more protected spaces on land?

Creating more protected spaces on land can be beneficial for conservation efforts and preserving biodiversity. Protected areas, such as national parks and nature reserves, can help to protect endangered species and their habitats, as well as provide recreational opportunities for people. However, it is also important to consider the potential impacts on local communities and their livelihoods, and to ensure that any protected areas are established and managed in an equitable and sustainable manner.

What are the most threatened large animal species?

There are many large animal species that are currently threatened with extinction. Some examples include:

Tigers, of which there are only an estimated 3,900 left in the wild.

African elephants, whose population has declined by about 30% in the last decade due to poaching.

Rhinoceroses, with all five species facing extinction due to poaching for their horns.

Gorillas and chimpanzees, whose populations are declining due to habitat loss and hunting.

Polar bears, whose sea ice habitat is being rapidly lost due to climate change.

Sea turtles, all seven species are endangered.

These are just a few examples, and there are many other large animal species that are also at risk of extinction. The main threats to large animal species include habitat loss, hunting and poaching, and climate change.

How is nature helping us fight climate change?

Nature can help us fight climate change in a few ways:
Carbon sequestration: Trees and other plants absorb carbon dioxide from the atmosphere and store it in their biomass. Forests, wetlands, and other natural habitats can act as "carbon sinks" and help to remove carbon dioxide from the atmosphere.

Methane reduction: Wetlands, peatlands, and other natural habitats can act as "methane sinks" by removing methane, a potent greenhouse gas, from the atmosphere.

Climate regulation: Ecosystems such as forests, oceans, and wetlands can help to regulate the Earth's climate by absorbing and storing carbon, releasing moisture, and influencing air and water temperatures.

Biodiversity conservation: Maintaining biodiversity can help to ensure the resilience of ecosystems and their ability to adapt to a changing climate.

Coastal protection: Natural habitats such as mangroves, salt marshes, and coral reefs can act as buffers against coastal erosion and storm surge, protecting coastal communities from the effects of sea-level rise and extreme weather.

It's worth noting that while nature can help us fight climate change, it's not a substitute for reducing emissions and transitioning to low-carbon energy sources. Human actions, mainly through the burning of fossil fuels, have been the main cause of climate change and need to be addressed through policies and actions to reduce greenhouse gas emissions.

How is nature fighting back against humans destroying the natural environment?

Nature can fight back against human destruction of the natural environment in a few ways:

90

Ecosystem resilience: Some ecosystems have the ability to recover from disturbances such as pollution or deforestation, and can adapt to changing conditions. For example, after a forest is cleared, new growth can emerge and eventually a new ecosystem can form.

Invasive species: When an ecosystem is disrupted, new species may move in and outcompete native species. This can lead to a loss of biodiversity, but can also result in the formation of a new ecosystem.

Climate change: As the climate changes, species and ecosystems will be forced to adapt or migrate to new areas. This can lead to changes in the distribution and abundance of species, and the formation of new ecosystems.

Natural disasters: Events such as hurricanes, floods, and fires can cause widespread destruction, but can also lead to new growth and the formation of new ecosystems.

It's worth noting that while nature can fight back against human destruction in some ways, it is not always able to recover fully or adapt fast enough to the human-caused destruction. Human actions have been altering ecosystems and causing extinctions at an unprecedented rate and scale, and the current rate of destruction is unsustainable.

How can we improve our society?

There are many ways to improve society, and different approaches may be more effective depending on the specific issues and contexts involved. Some possible strategies to consider include:

Promoting equality and inclusivity by addressing systemic discrimination and working to eliminate barriers that prevent marginalized groups from accessing opportunities and resources.

Investing in education, both to improve access to educational opportunities and to ensure that people are equipped with the knowledge and skills they need to succeed in the modern economy.

Providing access to healthcare, housing, and other basic necessities to ensure that everyone has the opportunity to live a healthy and fulfilling life.

Encouraging civic engagement and political participation, both to ensure that everyone's voices are heard and to hold elected officials accountable for their actions.

Investing in infrastructure and public services, such as transportation, clean energy, and internet access, to support economic growth and quality of life.

Encouraging sustainable economic growth by promoting innovation, entrepreneurship, and fair labor practices.

Reducing crime and violence by addressing root causes such as poverty, unemployment, and lack of education.

It's important to note that many of these solutions are interrelated, and addressing one issue will likely have positive impacts on others.

Is it likely that life as we know it could change drastically?

It is possible that life as we know it could change drastically in the future, due to a variety of factors such as natural disasters, technological advancements, economic and social changes, and political developments. Some examples of events or trends that could potentially lead to a drastic change in life as we know it include:

Climate change: The continued warming of the planet could lead to more frequent and severe extreme weather events, rising sea levels, and changes in precipitation patterns. These changes could have a significant impact on the availability of food and water, the spread of disease, and the displacement of people.

Technological advancements: The development of advanced technologies such as artificial intelligence, biotechnology, and nanotechnology could lead to radical changes in the way we live and work. It could also bring about new ethical and societal challenges, and could change the way we interact and communicate with each other.

Economic and social changes: Economic and social changes, such as increased inequality, shifting demographics, and changes in the nature of work, could lead to significant changes in the way we live and the way society is organized.

Political developments: Political developments, such as the emergence of new global powers, the rise of nationalism and extremist movements, and the erosion of democratic norms, could lead to significant changes in the global order and in the way nations interact with each other.

It's worth noting that, while some of these changes could bring about positive developments, such as new opportunities and advancements, they could also lead to negative consequences, such as increased conflict and suffering. Additionally, many of these changes are interconnected and could have a cascading effect on one another.

It's important to be aware of these potential developments and to strive to understand their implications, so that we can take steps to mitigate their negative effects and to take advantage of their positive effects.

What is quantum computing?

Quantum computing is a type of computing that is based on the principles of quantum physics, which describes the behavior of matter and energy at the atomic and subatomic level. Quantum computers use quantum bits, or qubits, which can exist in multiple states simultaneously, unlike classical bits in a traditional computer which can exist in two states (0 or 1) at any given time. This means that a quantum computer can perform certain types of calculations much faster than a classical computer.

Quantum computing has the potential to solve problems that are currently intractable for classical computers, such as breaking encryption codes, simulating complex chemical reactions, and optimizing large-scale logistics operations.

Quantum computing is still an active area of research, and there are currently different approaches being developed to build a quantum computer, such as superconducting qubits, trapped ions, and topological qubits. However, building a large-scale, practical, and stable quantum computer is still a big challenge, and it's not yet clear which technology will prove to be the most successful.

What can break the internet?

There are several potential scenarios that could lead to a widespread disruption of the internet, such as:

Cyber attacks: Malicious actors could launch large-scale attacks on internet infrastructure, such as servers, routers, and data centers, with the goal of disrupting or disabling internet services. Distributed denial-of-service (DDoS) attacks, in which a network of compromised devices is used to flood a target with traffic, can also bring down a website or a service.

Natural disasters: Extreme weather events, earthquakes, and other natural disasters can damage or destroy internet infrastructure, making it difficult or impossible for people in affected areas to access the internet.

Power outages: The internet relies on a vast network of servers and data centers that are powered by electricity, so a widespread power outage could cripple internet services.

Government censorship: Some governments have the capability to censor the internet by blocking websites, throttling traffic, or shutting down internet access altogether.

It's important to note that the internet is a vast and complex network that is distributed across the globe, so it would be difficult for any one event or action to completely "break" the internet. While a widespread disruption could certainly cause significant problems, it's likely that the internet would continue to function in some form, even if certain services or regions were affected. Additionally, the internet is designed to be resilient and able to adapt to changes, so it would be able to route around failures and to recover from a disruption.

What happens to society if the internet goes out?

If the internet were to suddenly go out, it would likely have a significant impact on society in a variety of ways. Some of the immediate effects could include:

Disruption of communication: The internet is the primary means of communication for many people, so a widespread outage would make it difficult or impossible for people to stay in touch with each other. This could have a particularly severe impact on people who rely on the internet for work, such as telecommuters, freelancers, and remote teams.

Loss of access to information: The internet is a vast repository of information, so a widespread outage would make it difficult or impossible for people to access news, entertainment, and other resources. This could have a particularly severe impact on people who rely on the internet for education, research, and other purposes.

Disruption of commerce: The internet is a vital tool for commerce, so a widespread outage would make it difficult or impossible for people to buy and sell goods and services. This could have a particularly severe impact on e-commerce, online marketplaces, and other businesses that rely on the internet.

Disruption of essential services: Many essential services such as banking, transportation, and healthcare rely on the internet for operation and communication, and a widespread internet outage would make it difficult or impossible for people to access these services.

In the long term, a widespread internet outage could lead to a variety of additional effects, such as a decline in economic productivity, a decline in social cohesion, and a decline in trust in technology. Additionally, it could lead to a further divide between those who have access to internet and those who don't, exacerbating the digital divide.

It's important to note that the internet is a critical infrastructure and its failure would have a severe impact on the society, thus it's important to have measures in place to ensure its continuity of operation.

Are we too reliant on the internet?

Many people today rely heavily on the internet for communication, information, entertainment, and a wide range of other activities. While the internet has brought many benefits, such as greater access to information, improved communication, and increased convenience, there are also concerns that we have become too reliant on it. Some of the potential downsides of our heavy reliance on the internet include:

Loss of privacy and security: As more and more information is shared and stored online, there is an increased risk of data breaches, hacking, and other forms of cybercrime. Additionally, the internet has made it easier for companies and governments to collect and analyze personal information.

Disruption of personal relationships: The internet has made it easier for people to connect with others, but it can also contribute to feelings of isolation, loneliness, and disconnection. Additionally, the internet can lead to a decline in face-to-face communication, which is important for maintaining relationships.

Disruption of traditional media: The internet has made it easier for people to access information and entertainment, but it has also led to a decline in traditional forms of media, such as newspapers and television. This could lead to a decline in the quality of journalism, a lack of diversity of voices, and a decline in the ability of people to access reliable information.

Disruption of critical thinking and attention span: The internet is filled with distractions and it's easy to get lost in the abundance of information. This can lead to a decline in critical thinking and attention span as people are easily overwhelmed by the vast amount of information available.

It's important to be aware of these potential downsides, and to strive for a balance between the benefits and the risks of our heavy reliance on the internet. This can include setting boundaries on technology use, making sure to spend time offline, and keeping an eye on the quality of information we consume.

Which parts of the world are best equipped to survive without the internet?

It's difficult to say which continents are best equipped to survive without the internet, as it would depend on a variety of factors such as the specific environment, the population's skills and knowledge, and access to resources. However, some continents may have an advantage over others in terms of their ability to survive without the internet.

For example, continents that have a significant portion of their population living in rural areas and engaged in subsistence farming or hunting and gathering, would likely be better equipped to survive without the internet. They are likely to have more experience in sourcing their needs from the environment, and have a greater understanding of the local flora and fauna.

Continents with a long history of traditional cultures, such as Africa, Asia, and the Americas, may also be better equipped to survive without the internet, as they may have a deeper understanding of traditional knowledge and skills that are necessary to survive in a wilderness setting.

Similarly, regions with a long history of self-sufficiency and resilience, such as the Arctic and the Antarctic, may also be better equipped to survive without the internet. They are often isolated and have to be self-sufficient due to lack of infrastructure and access to resources.

It's important to note that the ability to survive without the internet would also depend on the specific environment, the resources available, and the population's physical and mental condition. Additionally, not all rural areas or traditional cultures are the same, some regions may have more resources or better infrastructure to support the population.

Would people be able to survive in the wild?

It's difficult to estimate the exact percentage of people who would not be able to survive in the wild, as it would depend on a variety of factors such as the specific environment, the individual's skills and knowledge, and access to resources. However, it is likely that the majority of people living in modern societies would have difficulty surviving in a wilderness setting without access to modern technology and infrastructure.

Most people in modern societies have grown up in an environment where their basic needs for food, shelter, and warmth are met by the systems in place and are not accustomed to finding and sourcing those needs through nature. Additionally, many people do not have the knowledge, skills, or physical ability to find food, build shelter, or start a fire in a wilderness setting. People also may not have the ability to navigate, orient or even recognize the natural signs of weather or seasons.

It's worth noting that the ability to survive in the wild is not only determined by an individual's knowledge and skills but also by the environment, the resources available, and the individual's physical and mental condition. Furthermore, not all wilderness environments are the same, some places are harsher and more challenging than others, it also depends on the time of the year.

In any case, it is important to note that survival in the wild should not be taken lightly, it requires knowledge, skill, and the proper equipment. It's always recommended to seek guidance from professionals and have the proper training before venturing into the wilderness.

Can AI solve all of our problems?

Artificial intelligence (AI) has the potential to solve many problems, but it is not a panacea for all issues. The capabilities of AI systems are limited by the quality of the data they are trained on, the algorithms used to build them, and the resources available to run them. Additionally, many problems, such as those related to ethics and values, may be difficult or impossible for AI to solve without human input. It is important to understand the limitations and capabilities of AI in order to effectively utilize it to solve problems.

What are some problems that AI cannot solve?

There are several types of problems that AI may not be able to solve, including:

Ethical and moral dilemmas: AI systems can make decisions based on data, but they cannot yet understand or evaluate ethical principles and values.

Creativity: While AI can generate new ideas and designs, it lacks the ability to truly be creative in the same way that humans can be.

Understanding context: AI may struggle with understanding the nuances and subtleties of human communication and social context.

Common sense: AI systems lack the kind of "common sense" understanding of the world that humans take for granted, which makes it difficult for AI to navigate real-world situations.

Emotions: AI systems do not have emotions, and have a hard time understanding or dealing with them.

Open-ended problems: AI excels at solving well-defined problems with clear goals, but struggles with problems that do not have clear solutions or that require novel approaches.

These are just a few examples, and the field of AI is rapidly evolving, so the limitations of AI may change over time as the technology advances.

How many people use AI programs every day?

It is difficult to estimate the exact number of people who use AI programs every day, as it can vary widely depending on the definition of "AI program" and the methods used to measure usage. However, it is safe to say that AI is becoming increasingly prevalent in our daily lives, and its usage is growing rapidly. Some examples of AI programs that many people use every day include:

Virtual assistants like Siri, Alexa, and Google Assistant.

Smartphone apps that use AI for tasks such as image recognition, natural language processing, and personalization

Social media platforms that use AI for tasks such as content recommendations, moderation, and targeted advertising

Online shopping platforms that use AI for tasks such as product recommendations and search results

Navigation and map apps that use AI for tasks such as traffic predictions and route optimization

Email and messaging apps that use AI for tasks such as spam filtering and automated responses

Banking apps and websites that use AI for tasks such as fraud detection and account management.

As technology continues to evolve and AI is becoming more mainstream, the number of people using AI programs every day is likely to increase.

Do AI programs contribute to misinformation?

AI can be used to both contribute to and combat misinformation. On one hand, AI can be used to generate deepfake videos and images, as well as to create fake social media accounts and bots that can spread misinformation at scale. On the other hand, AI can be used to detect and flag false information, and to help fact-checkers and journalists verify the accuracy of news and information.

However, AI is not neutral and it learns from the dataset it was trained on. If the dataset is biased, the AI model will also learn and propagate the bias. As such, it's important that the data used to train AI models is diverse and unbiased, and that the models are evaluated and tested for fairness and accuracy.

It is also important to note that AI is not a magic bullet, it can assist and help but it's not a replacement for human judgement and critical thinking. The best way to combat misinformation is through a combination of AI-assisted tools and human oversight and analysis.

What would our world look like without AI?

A world without AI would be very different from the one we currently live in. Many of the technologies and systems that we rely on today, such as smartphones, search engines, self-driving cars, and virtual assistants, would not exist. Industries such as finance, transportation, healthcare, and manufacturing would have to function without the use of AI algorithms and automation.

In terms of everyday life, tasks that are currently done by AI such as online shopping, language translation, and image recognition would have to be done manually. Some of the benefits of AI such as improved efficiency, increased accuracy and convenience would be lost.

Additionally, the research and development of AI would not have progressed as it has, so many of the advancements in fields such as natural language processing, computer vision, and machine learning would not have occurred. This could have a major impact on the overall progress of technology and science.

Overall, a world without AI would be much less advanced and efficient than the world we live in today.

What was our world like before AI?

Before the development of AI, the world was primarily driven by manual labor and human decision-making. Many tasks that are now done by AI were done by humans, such as data analysis, customer service, and repetitive manual tasks.

In terms of technology, computers existed but their capabilities were limited compared to today. They were primarily used for basic calculations and data storage, and were not capable of tasks such as natural language processing and image recognition.

In terms of industry, automation was limited to simple mechanical processes. Robotics were not as advanced, and many processes were done by human workers.

In terms of everyday life, people relied on human-made products and services, such as maps, encyclopedias, and customer service. People also spent more time on repetitive tasks such as doing calculations, finding information and organizing data.

Overall, the world before AI was less advanced, less efficient, and less interconnected than it is today. The advancements in AI have had a significant impact on technology, industry, and everyday life.

What was life like before the internet?

Life without the internet was very different from what it is today. The internet, as we know it, became widely available in the 1990s, so before that time, people had to rely on other means to access information, communicate with others, and conduct business. Here are a few examples of how life was different without the internet.

Access to information: Without the internet, people had to rely on books, newspapers, television, and radio to access information. This meant that the information available was often more limited and less up-to-date than what is available today.

Communication: Without the internet, people had to rely on phone calls, letters, and in-person visits to communicate with others. This made it more difficult to stay in touch with people who lived far away, and it was not possible to have real-time communication with people from all over the world.

Entertainment: Without the internet, people had to rely on television, radio, and movies to be entertained. There were fewer options for streaming content and people had to rely on physical media such as VHS tapes, CDs, and DVD to watch movies or listen to music.

Shopping: Without the internet, people had to rely on physical stores to buy goods, and didn't have the option to shop online. This made it more difficult to find a wide range of products, and often meant that people had to travel long distances to find what they were looking for.

Research: Without the internet, research was more time-consuming, difficult, and less efficient. People had to rely on physical libraries, books, and journals to conduct research.

Overall, life without the internet was less connected, less efficient and less convenient. The internet has revolutionized the way we live and work, and it has become an essential part of daily life for many people.

Can we ever go back to life without the internet?

It's unlikely that we will ever go back to life without the internet. The internet has become an integral part of many aspects of modern life, and it has revolutionized the way we communicate, access information, conduct business, and entertain ourselves. The internet and the digital technologies that have come along with it have changed the way we live, work, and interact with one another.

While it's possible that internet access and availability could be disrupted in certain areas or during certain periods of time, such as during a widespread power outage or in the event of a natural disaster, it's unlikely that the internet will disappear entirely. The internet is a decentralized network of networks, and it's designed to be resilient and able to adapt to changes. Even if internet access is disrupted in one area, there are likely to be other areas where access is still available.

Furthermore, the internet has brought about many positive developments, such as greater access to information, improved communication, and increased convenience. It's unlikely that people would want to give up these benefits, even if it meant returning to a pre-internet way of life.

It's worth noting, however, that it's important to be aware of the potential downsides of heavy reliance on the internet, and to strive for a balance between the benefits and the risks of our heavy reliance on the internet. This can include setting boundaries on technology use, making sure to spend time offline, and keeping an eye on the quality of information we consume.

If all humans could unite, what should we put our collective efforts towards?

If all humans were able to unite, there are a number of important issues that we could work on together. Some of the most pressing global challenges facing humanity include:

Climate change: The Earth's climate is changing rapidly due to human activities such as burning fossil fuels and deforestation. If all humans united, we could work together to reduce our greenhouse gas emissions, shift to renewable energy sources, and protect vulnerable communities from the impacts of climate change.

Poverty and inequality: Despite tremendous progress in recent decades, there are still billions of people living in poverty around the world. If all humans united, we could work together to ensure that everyone has access to basic needs like food, shelter, and healthcare.

Disease: The COVID-19 pandemic has highlighted the importance of global health, but there are many other diseases that affect millions of people worldwide. If all humans united, we could work together to fund research and develop treatments and vaccines for a wide range of diseases

Conflict: Wars and civil conflicts cause immense suffering and displacement around the world. If all humans united, we could work together to promote peace, disarmament, and reconciliation.

Education and literacy: Education is key to breaking the cycle of poverty and promoting economic growth. If all humans united, we could work together to provide quality education to all children, regardless of where they live or how much money their families have.

Sustainability: Ensuring that human populations can thrive without causing long-term damage to the planet is crucial. This includes addressing issues such as climate change, deforestation, pollution and loss of biodiversity.

Equity: Ensuring that all people have access to the resources and opportunities they need to thrive. This includes addressing issues such as poverty, hunger, and lack of access to healthcare and education.

Peace: Working to prevent and resolve conflicts and promote cooperation between nations, communities and individuals.

Science and technology: Investing in research and development of new technologies and innovations to improve human life and address global challenges.

Health: Investing in public health and healthcare, and working to address global health challenges such as pandemics, chronic diseases and mental health.

Human rights: Advancing and protecting the rights and dignity of all people, regardless of gender, race, religion, sexual orientation, or any other characteristic.

It is important to note that these are not exclusive and are interconnected.